Linda Viktoria Andersson

Plato's Political Imagination

Linda Viktoria Andersson

Plato's Political Imagination

The Imagination as Both Philosophical and Democratically Political

VDM Verlag Dr. Müller

Imprint

Bibliographic information by the German National Library: The German National Library lists this publication at the German National Bibliography; detailed bibliographic information is available on the Internet at http://dnb.d-nb.de.

Any brand names and product names mentioned in this book are subject to trademark, brand or patent protection and are trademarks or registered trademarks of their respective holders. The use of brand names, product names, common names, trade names, product descriptions etc. even without a particular marking in this works is in no way to be construed to mean that such names may be regarded as unrestricted in respect of trademark and brand protection legislation and could thus be used by anyone.

Cover image: www.purestockx.com

Publisher:
VDM Verlag Dr. Müller Aktiengesellschaft & Co. KG, Dudweiler Landstr. 125 a, 66123 Saarbrücken, Germany,
Phone +49 681 9100-698, Fax +49 681 9100-988,
Email: info@vdm-verlag.de

Copyright © 2008 VDM Verlag Dr. Müller Aktiengesellschaft & Co. KG and licensors
All rights reserved. Saarbrücken 2008

Produced in USA and UK by:
Lightning Source Inc., La Vergne, Tennessee, USA
Lightning Source UK Ltd., Milton Keynes, UK
BookSurge LLC, 5341 Dorchester Road, Suite 16, North Charleston, SC 29418, USA

ISBN: 978-3-639-00494-6

Table of Contents

I. Introduction: Political Imagination   1

-Political Imagination   3
-Approach   6
-Organization   9

II. Image-Making and Imagination in the *Republic*   9

-Imagination   9
-Images in the Republic   10
-Founders and Philosophers   11
-Image-Making   12
-The Divided Line   14

III. Images in Education and Poetry   20

-Education and Poetry   20
-Children's Images and Play   21
- The Tyrant   24
- Images in Logos   24
- Bad Images: Tragedy and Human Agency   27
- Good Images   32
- Stinging and Numbing Education for the Soul   34

IV. Images: Democracy and the Ideal   37

- Ideal and Democracy   37
- City in speech: the Just City   38
- The Sun: child of the Good   43
- Weaving the Good Life   46
- Democracy: Collective Image-Making   48
- Criticism and Democracy   51

V. Conclusion   53

VI. Bibliography   55

Acknowledgments

I would like to thank my academic advisor, Professor Christina Tarnopolsky. Her comments, criticisms, and questions have been invaluable. I could not have written this thesis without her help and sincere dedication. I would also thank my boyfriend Randall Jonas, and my family, for supporting and encouraging me.

I. Introduction: Political Imagination

Political Imagination

This paper seeks to explore and discuss the political role of the imagination in Plato. What is the role of the imagination in the *Republic*? How does it relate to reason and notions of the ideal? And what role does it play in philosophy and politics; in poetry and rhetoric? I will argue that Plato does not view the imagination as wholly negative or of a low status. Rather, the imagination contains both positive and negative aspects which Plato is acutely aware of. Thus, I will not pursue an argument that seeks to illustrate, for instance, that Plato is anti-imagination and therefore is an anti-romantic or austere censor of everything imaginative. Part of the aim of this project is to highlight both negative and positive aspects in Plato's treatment of the imagination, in order to understand the **political** roles of the imagination more generally.

But can it be argued that there is **political** imagination in the *Republic?* If one takes the view that the imagination presented in the *Republic* is cognition and judgement free, that it is, wholly of sense and not of mind, then the notion that the imagination is political, and therefore important, may seem preposterous[1]. However, rejecting the reading which assigns an inferior status to the imagination, I will argue that the *political* and *social* role of the imagination is more dynamic and hopeful in Plato than one may expect[2]. On my reading, the imagination is central for Plato as a writer of drama and philosophy: he uses images and poetry (myths, stories) in his dialogues. In this sense, he is both a philosopher and a poet. However, the dialectical project in Plato's dialogues **also** provides a large role for the imagination, not only for the philosopher (Socrates or Plato) but for the other participants as well. Hence I will seek to argue that there is an extensive amount of political imagination through image-making and imaginative identification, in the *Republic*.

---

[1] This interpretation relies heavily on the "lowly" status of images and imagination on the Divided Line. For an example of this view see Ray Hart's article "Imagination in Plato" *International Philosophical Quarterly* Vol. V (1965) 436-46.
[2] In the *Republic* poets are banned from the just city. This does not seem to provide the imagination with much of a political or social role.

Further, image-making has both important educative and democratic features and functions. For example, even if Socrates, on his own, reasons without images, which may or may not be the case, he does not discuss or educate without images. In addition, the **process** of constructing the ideal in the *Republic* illustrates the **collective** nature of image-making. Socrates, Glaucon and Adeimantus construct the city in speech *together*. And this particular ideal is pursued due to the explicit wishes of Socrates' interlocutors who want to know what justice looks like on its own. I will argue that this indicates that Socratic discussion has important democratic aspects, and that the use of images and image-making is an important part of this form of discussion[3]. Image-making is not only a solitary practice reserved for the inspired genius, philosopher, artist or politician. Rather, in the *Republic*, images are constructed, modified and judged collectively **in speech**.

However, it could be objected that even if there are images created and put to use in the *Republic*; this does not necessarily imply that there ought to be imagination and images in politics, in general? In other words, how is the treatment of images in the *Republic* politically relevant to us? In my view, though, images are crucial for a politics that seeks to engage in the mediation of the actual and the ideal. For instance, a vision or a reasoned premise about a different society needs to *capture the imagination* of politicians and citizens alike in order to be compelling. On the other hand, it is also through an elaborate image of the ideal in speech, interpreted and judged by reason, that one may gain an understanding of the dangers of taking one specific ideal notion, such as equality or justice, to its extreme. In other words, one may not be able to foresee the drastic possibilities inherent in a premise or an idea until one draws out its implications by way of constructing an image, such as an ideal city, with others, in discussion. I would therefore argue that the *Republic* has much to teach politics: it illustrates the constant interplay between the actual and the ideal; between images and judgment, and it emphasizes the importance of speech and dialogue in politics in general. Therefore, it is

---

[3] With democratic aspects here I refer to the specific mode of philosophic discussion. Discussion is connected to a notion of democracy because it is open-ended, participatory, active and dynamic. It is not authoritarian, and rigid.

because this sort of discussion employs images that the act of imagining in this particular context can be said to be both relevant and political.

Still, it should be emphasized that I do not seek to argue that the imagination is *only good* for Plato. Part of the strength of Plato's discussion of the imagination is that it also looks to its negative aspects. For example, images, stories or myths unaccompanied by rational argumentation are not useful. In other words, the objects produced by the imagination have to be anchored by rational argumentation: one has to be capable of giving an account of one's images in speech (*logos*). If I cannot give an account of an image or story which I present, or allow it to be questioned, criticized and "tested" then it has little philosophical or ethical value, regardless of how beautiful it may or may not be. The skilled sophist or poet who does not remind the audience that he is indeed providing them with images, rather than the 'real' or the actual, is deceptive. Politically this is dangerous because it divorces speech from truth and truthfulness: all that matters is the ability to persuade an audience with attractive images which they take for the truth[4]. Yet, even more dangerous than the deceptive sophist, is the person who *imagines* himself to be just, good, or noble when in fact he is not. This type of "false" imagining is wholly divorced from critical self-distance, and this type of person is not of a sound mind: he is detached from reasonable discourse and action. This may be the case with a poet claiming to be reporting straight from the gods. By contrast, Socrates **reminds** his interlocutors that they are making an image, or that *all* he can do is to give them an image. Instead of dazzling or his audience by inducing "blind" faith, Socrates aims at fostering scepticism and criticism. Thus he also continuously reminds us of the impossibility of effortlessly reproduce in deed that which is produced in speech (473a)[5]: an image *cannot* come to be perfectly in 'reality'.

How images are used is therefore immensely important, much more important than trying to determine the winner in the "battle" between reason and imagination. Plato's dialogues

---

[4] Of course this may suffice for someone who believes that politics should indeed only be concerned with persuasion and that which people are prone to believe.
[5] Plato *The Republic* intro., trans., and notes by Allan Bloom (New York: Basic Books), 1968.
Please note that hereafter all references, unless other wise indicated, from the *Republic* will come from this translation and all numerical references are to the Stephanus pages.

display a fluid interplay between stunningly beautiful images, and more mundane questioning, division, classification and rational argumentation. In the dialogues we see that discussion and deliberation involves both *logos* (speech*)* and *muthos* (stories*,* myths), reason and imagination. One without the other is not good, and the critical issue at stake is to search for a beneficial balance and correct usage of both.

Approach

A "traditional" reading of Plato's texts often makes Socrates Plato's mouthpiece. Socrates "gives" us the truth: he gives us Plato's doctrine[6]. On this reading Plato may frequently come out as an authoritarian, after all, he does for instance, create a highly restrictive *Kallipolis* in the *Republic*. Further, Socrates' interlocutors are often all too lame to offer any real critique or challenge to Socrates[7]. Therefore one may be tempted to conclude that we do not need to pay too much attention to them since they mostly just agree with Socrates. This paper will **not** provide such a traditional or "literal" reading[8]. However, this does not mean that I dismiss the many valuable insights reached through this mode of interpretation; or more importantly, that I do not take the texts seriously. I do not think much would be gained by dismissing the dialogues as jokes or pure irony. But, if one is looking for a "philosophic need for democracy in Plato's writings"[9] one will not find it in the tradition of literal interpretation. In this tradition it is hard to get beyond Plato the authoritarian.

Secondly, it should be noted that this paper will not partake in the chronological dispute regarding the correct order of Plato's dialogues. Thus, I will not base my arguments on claims that Plato came to change his view of the role of images and the imagination: that he, for example, went from anti-imagination in the *Republic* to pro-imagination in the *Timaeus*. This may indeed be the case, but it is very hard to know for sure. Indeed if one compares the *Laws* to the *Symposium*, one may wonder if the same person could have

---

[6] John E., Peterman *On Plato* (Belmont, CA: Wadsworth), 2000, p53.
[7] However, this is not always the case: for instance, the Pythagorean interlocutors in the *Phaedo* are quite skilled.
[8] With literal I refer to a reading which extrapolates Socrates' statements from the text in order to add them up to a logical "doctrine". This type of reading tends to overlook the dramatic form of the Platonic dialogues. On my reading one needs to take the entire dialogue into account: its setting, its characters etc.
[9] Peterman, *On Plato* 2000, p53.

possibly written both texts. Again, we do not know for sure. Therefore it is not within the scope of this paper to try to entangle and weigh in on the chronological debate. Instead I will seek to engage directly with each text.

Further, I will not argue for a distinct split between the Socratic and the Platonic in the dialogues. I do not see Socrates only as Plato's mouthpiece, nor do I think that in some dialogues Plato was merely "recording" or reporting on what Socrates said. Plato's Socrates is a fictional creation: exactly how true to the historical Socrates is very difficult for us to ever know. Indeed, this dilemma about our access to the past is highlighted by Plato: in the *Symposium* we do not get a first-hand account or "live" reporting of the events at Agathon's house. Instead we get a story pieced together from gossip, and second-hand accounts told a long time after the actual event. Even the *Republic* is told by Socrates a day *after* the actual conversation. To expect to perfectly separate "real" Socrates from Plato's or Xenophon's is in my view not possible. And since I am not engaged in dividing and classifying the dialogues I hope that I can continue without having to try to do so[10].

Organization
This paper is divided into three main sections. The first part discusses the different features of images and image-making in the *Republic*. Put briefly, it argues that there are three central aspects of the imagination in the *Republic*: the construction of images, the pretending to be a founder, and the identification with the philosopher. I will discuss the role of the imagination in the *Republic* in *all* the various images used by Socrates (i.e. the Cave, the Good etc) in the construction of the ideal in speech.

The second part discusses the relationship between images, art, education, and *logos*. Firstly, it seeks to distinguish between good and bad images in children's education and in poetry. The banning of the poets in Book 10 of the *Republic* will be central, but I will also draw upon Book 2 and 3 of the *Republic*, as well as on examples from *Meno* and the

---

[10] I will always use "Socrates" if I am discussing a particular quote or myth presented by him. I will use Plato when I speak more generally.

Symposium. In short, it seeks to argue that the poet, when attacked by Plato, is frequently bunched together with the sophist as a dealer in deceptive images and illusions[11]. However, not all art is therefore bad: I will argue that Plato, in fact, holds the more fantastical' images as more useful than the materialistic or realistic ones. Secondly, the role of images in logos is discussed by a focus on the necessity of blending or weaving of images and rational argumentation in speech. It discusses the relationship between *muthos* and *logos*. Finally, I conclude this section by arguing that images, stories and myths, "awake" a passion in us and open us up to the possibility of beauty in the search and striving for knowledge. In other words, the images impress themselves upon us, and engage us emotionally.

Finally, the last section addresses the notion of the ideal. I will discuss the Just City, (the city in speech) in the *Republic* and I will seek to address the question of *where* and *what* the ideal is. On my reading, the ideal is linked to images and democracy through the process of discussion, inquiry and criticism. That is, discussion provokes an imaginative **vision** *(theoria)* of the ideal: for instance, an image of oneself perfected, or the possibility of self-knowledge and well-being of the soul. In so far as the ideal thus comes to life in speech it is not remote or inaccessible. Lastly, image-making and democracy are linked to philosophy. Socrates makes and presents images in discussion with others, and he is willing to discuss with anyone who cares to take the time to stop and listen. I will end by discussing why there is a need for democracy in philosophy, and how this need is illustrated by Plato.

---

[11] This may lead one to wonder if the quarrel is not only between philosophy and poetry, but also between philosophy and sophistry. In both cases philosophy needs to show how it is not the same as either poetry or sophistry.

II. Image-Making and Imagination in the *Republic*

Imagination

Before embarking on any discussion of the imagination one may one wonder if it is indeed appropriate to do so considering the fact that the specific word is only used twice in the *Republic*?[12] This has led scholars to question if Plato did in fact have any relevant sense of the imagination as we think of it today[13]. However, while I do not underestimate the seriousness of this objection, I would still question whether a strictly literal approach is the most useful in this case. For example, few would, I believe, disagree with the fact that the dialogue in the *Republic* is dramatic, and therefore imaginative, and that the characters in the *Republic* imagine various scenarios and images together. Thus, even if the specific word is not used, the text is full of references to images, image-making and pretending. In my view, it would therefore be unfortunate if one chooses not to engage in a discussion of the imagination and its objects and processes, simply because the word itself is very rarely used.

Nevertheless, one most certainly has to be aware of the fact that the imagination did not mean the same thing to the Greeks as it does to us. With romanticism comes an almost unlimited belief in the goodness of the imagination, and we often think of it as a separate mental faculty, divorced from reason and emotion. Plato clearly did not regard the imagination, or more importantly its objects, to be in any exclusive faculty of their own. And this is why, as Stephen Halliwell argues, Plato does not shy away from stating that images should also be held "ethically accountable"[14] because they can have very transformative effects on us. That is, images are not neutral or normative-free. And in my view, it is precisely because Plato does not assign the imagination any special all-good or value-free status that he is so relevant to us today: rather than seeing the imagination as an unquestionable good, Plato helps us to see both its negative and positive aspects and uses. What's more, by assigning a normative accountability to images such as those

---

[12] The *Republic*, the Greek word in Bloom's translation is *eikasia* and it appears in passages 511e and 534a.
[13] Stephen Halliwell, "Plato, Imagination and Romanticism" *The Passionate Intellect: Essays on the Transformation of the Classical Tradition,* ed. L. Ayres (New Brunswick, NJ: Transaction Publishers) 1995, pp23-37, p27.

[14] Halliwell, "Plato, Imagination and Romanticism" pp23-37, p36.

produced in art, Plato not only recognizes how powerful images can be; he also urges us to think of art, politics and philosophy as closely interconnected.

Keeping in mind then the fact that this paper is mainly focused on the objects produced by the imagination, i.e. images, I hope it will be sufficiently clear what I mean, even when I use the word imagination itself[15]. As stated earlier, I deal with the *political* uses of the imagination and images. Thus, I am not concerned with the issue of when we imagine and when we reason on our own, or whether an idea precedes an image or if all ideas are images. I will not discuss **how** Socrates came to "see" or possess the image of the cave, only that he employs it to explain and teach. Further, I will stress the *interconnectedness* of reason and imagination; of images and judgment, in speech, and political discussion.

Images in the Republic
Why are images used at all in the *Republic*? Why can't Socrates state what he wishes to find out and explain about justice, with the sole use of reasoned premises, arguments and refutations? In Book 1 of the Republic this is essentially what takes place: Socrates refutes his interlocutors incessantly, in order to prove how insufficient their various definitions of justice are. However, this does not leave his interlocutors at all satisfied, and Thrasymachus charges: "if you truly want to know what the just is, don't only ask and gratify your love of honor by refuting whatever someone answers" (336c) This is briefly after Socrates has even "succeeded" in making Thrasymachus blush (350d).By the end of Book 1 it is clear that Socrates' method is not working. It is not constructive because it leaves the audience, frustrated, and angry, and in Thrasymachus' case, insulted and defeated. And, Socrates is not content either: "I am just like the gluttons who grab at

---

[15] For instance, I may refer to "Plato's discussion of the imagination" even though he explicitly does not discuss the imagination in this fashion. However, he does discuss images and their psychological effects on us. In "Plato, Imagination and Romanticism" 1995, Stephen Halliwell argues that because Plato is concerned with the psychological effects of images on us he did come to a "realization of some of the workings of the imagination", p26-27. I agree with this reading. It should also be noted that the word imagination comes from the Latin *imaginary* meaning "picture to oneself" and *imago* meaning image. See *Oxford Concise Dictionary*. The idea of "picture to oneself" might suggest that the *solitary* aspects we now associate with imagination is foreign to Plato's understanding, and that this too is helpful for developing a political notion of the imagination.

whatever is set before them to get a taste of it, before they have in proper measure enjoyed what went before" (345b). Socrates has gorged himself on rational argumentation and in the end no-one is any wiser for it. Productive inquiry and discussion does therefore appear to require a different approach, which amongst other things, establishes a friendlier and less hostile atmosphere amongst its participants. What follows in many respects can be regarded as an imaginative political journey into the nature of justice and injustice.

Founders and Philosophers

This journey begins by Socrates asking his interlocutors to **pretend** to be founders of a city: "Come now" I said "let's make a city in speech from the beginning" (369c). This act of pretending will help them locate justice, the argument being that if they can manage to see justice in a city then they will also be able to identify it in the soul of an individual. The act of pretending is political because they are not imagining just **any** thing: they are founding **a city** in speech, and they are searching for **justice**. The pretending also produces imaginative identification: Glaucon and Adeimantus are not crafting a city by remaining, so to speak, themselves. Rather, by putting themselves in the shoes of a founder, they are forced to take overall and general concerns of the wellbeing of the entire city, into account. One implication of this exercise is to bring them closer to philosophy and politics: the founding of a city requires them to turn away from private and personal concerns and instead think in more general and public terms. In order to stay on track with their task at hand, they need to *remember* to remain founders throughout the discussion, as Socrates at one point cautions Adeimantus: "Adeimantus, you and I are not poets right now but founders of a city" (369c). They must avoid getting bogged down by the particular concerns of different professions, if they are to be successful founders. And if they cannot found a city in speech they cannot find out what justice is. In my view it is not accidental that Socrates has Glaucon and Adeimantus search for justice **in** the political. It is not only that a city is 'bigger' than an individual soul. It also indicates a crucial connection between the ideal and the political, between the political and the ethical.

Once the city in speech is constructed, they have completed their task as founders. Yet their work is not finished. They now have to **find** justice in the city (427e). By agreeing to continue the journey with Socrates, Glaucon and Adeimantus are even more closely able to identify themselves with the philosopher. They are to become acquainted with the philosophical method of searching for something by ruling out that which it is **not**. And in doing so, Glaucon and Adeimantus are learning what it means to be philosophers.

Image-Making
As argued above the main collectively crafted image in the *Republic*, is the image of the city in speech. Socrates does not simply feed his audience with a complete ready-made image of a city. Instead Adeimantus and Socrates start by crafting the city of necessity. However, this city does not satisfy Glaucon who sees it as too austere: why couldn't the inhabitants have relishes, couches etc? And Socrates remarks: "I understand. We are, as it seems, considering not only how a city, but also a luxurious city, comes into being. Perhaps that's not bad either" (427e). From there they go on to craft the feverish city; which they later purge. The point here is that the image is crafted *together*, and as this process goes on the city in speech is modified and reworked over and over. I would argue that this is an indication of both the central position of images in the discussion, and the democratic aspects of image-making and discussion more generally. Discussion, as opposed to long speeches, is inherently dynamic and democratic: we do not know exactly where we will end up when we engage in discussion. We can object, modify and add to what others have said before. In short, we can participate actively. Recall that Socrates, Glaucon and Adeimantus pretend to be founders of a city together. This imaginary founding in which all three participate might be the only case of *democratic* founding in Athenian history.

Nevertheless it could be argued that the whole effort of crafting the city in speech is *really* all Socrates' doing. In other words, even though the others take part in the discussion Socrates decides where it is going and crafts the image entirely to his own liking. He only makes it *appear* as if they are doing it together because it is a more effective way of persuading and teaching someone, rather than commanding or preaching to them. While I do not deny the educative intentions of Socrates' method I would still contend that he himself is not always aware of where the discussion is taking them. For example, in debating the possibility of the just city, and if it is the best city; Socrates is pressed by his interlocutors to **tell** them but he says: "But to present arguments at a time when one is in doubt and seeking….is a thing both frightening and slippery" (451a). On my reading Socrates is not being falsely modest here: he is not reluctant to admit that he does not know. However, he is reluctant to present arguments when this is the case. And previously when deciding what sort of poetry they shall allow in the city Socrates says: "Perhaps, and perhaps something still more than this. You see, I myself really don't know yet" (394d). The dialogue thus exposes some of Socrates own perplexities and that he does not pretend to have any ultimate or definite answers. Furthermore, at the beginning of Book 5 Polemarchus, who whispers to Adeimantus, has Socrates revise his previous account: he is forced to include eros (449b-c). Socrates has tried to sneak in the communalization of eros, i.e. the idea that love and sex should be communal rather than private, as something very ordinary, but Polemarchus will not accept his account. This is an example of Socrates **not** deciding and dictating the entire dialogue. In fact, as David Roochnik argues, it is **Glaucon** who is largely responsible for the "forward momentum of the *Republic*. His energy, his passion for the conversation, his forcefulness, and his crucial insights are necessary goads for an otherwise reluctant Socrates"[16].

Still, not all images are collectively crafted in the *Republic*; some appear to be presented by Socrates because they are the only way possible for him to illustrate what he means. For instance, when Adeimantus wonders why philosophers should rule since they were previously charged with uselessness, Socrates answers: "The question you are asking needs an answer given through an image" (487e). Glaucon then observes that this must be hard for Socrates since he is not used to speaking in images, but Socrates does not agree, instead he asks if Glaucon is making fun of him and then he goes on to say: "At all events, listen to the image so you may still see how greedy I am for images"(487e). But why does Socrates *need* to give his answer through an image? Why can't he more plainly

---

[16]David Roochnik, *Beautiful City: The Dialectical Character of Plato's Republic* (Ithaca, New York: Cornell University Press) 2003, p56.

explain that the philosophers are misunderstood? Socrates says that they have indeed involved him "in an argument so hard to prove" (487e-488a), which may indicate that the he can indeed only answer through an image or a story. However, this may not be the case, but regardless of whether Socrates *could* have addressed the charge of philosophers being useless without an image, I believe that the story about the philosopher in Book 6, provides us with a more vivid and striking impression of the fate of philosophy than a more plain answer ever could. This is why the answer **needs** an image.

The image Socrates goes on to give Glaucon and Adeimantus is the story of the "rather deaf and likewise somewhat short-sighted" (488b-c) ship-owner, who has poor skills in piloting his ship. While most of the crew tries to flatter and praise the ship-owner to win his favour, the true pilot gets slandered as a star gazer (488c-d). Socrates concludes by telling Glaucon to "teach the image to that man who wonders at the philosophers not being honoured in the cities" (489a). And to *teach* this image in discussion does seem, to me, to be a very effective way of communicating an important counter-argument to those who charge philosophers with being useless. Further, the underlying assumption Plato exposes here is that it is commonly thought that philosophy does not deal in images: most likely it is somehow perceived that philosophy first and foremost deals in reasoned arguments. Plato shows us that philosophy **does** deal in images: the journey in the *Republic* is full of extraordinary ones such as the Three Waves, the Cave, the Sun and Er's trip to the underworld, to name a few.

The Divided Line

The more "standard" accounts of the treatment of the imagination in the *Republic*, as previously mentioned, draw almost exclusively on what Socrates says about the imagination and its objects and where he places it on the divided line. The interpretations which claim that Plato regards images and the imagination as "lowly" do so because Socrates in Book 6, places them at the bottom of the divided line, which is regarded as a ladder depicting the ascent to true knowledge. The different steps of the ladder signify increasing levels of cognitive activity, and since the imagination is at the very bottom it has no cognition, no judgement or distinction between true-false or reality-unreality[17].

---

[17] Hart "Imagination in Plato", 1965 p444.

To be sure it is the *foundation* for cognition, trust and knowledge; but as a first step it is something to be overcome and left behind[18]. True knowledge is freed from untrustworthy images and imaginings. This reading places great emphasis on the divided line because it believes that it is here that Plato gives us an important part of his "Theory of Ideas" or "Theory of knowledge".

Against this background a discussion of images in the *Republic* needs to examine the image of the divided line extra carefully even if it is only one of many central images in the text. To briefly recapitulate the basic structure of this image: the two central segments of the divided line correspond to the *intelligible* and the *visible*. The objects of the visible section are images (*eikones*), followed by their originals i.e. objects of sense such as plants, animals etc. (509d-510a)The corresponding mode of thinking used to discern these objects are imagination and trust. The objects of the intelligible area are mathematical objects, followed by forms (*eide*), and its modes of thinking are thought and intellection (510b).

On my reading, the divided line illustrates that some knowledge is visible: we use our senses to judge concrete objects and things, or images of concrete objects and things, such as plants, animals etc. Other knowledge is referred to as intelligible: it focuses on that which we know through *nous* (mind). We turn to this type of knowledge when our senses cannot provide any clear-cut answers, as when something is both, in Plato's language, one and many at the same time. The Divided line is hence focused on the *distinction* between what we know through senses and what we know through mind. Images have clearly suffered because they are placed in the visible section: however it should be remembered that, the **specific** images referred to here are images of actual, material objects, not **all** possible images. To me this suggests that images and the imagination do not only operate in the area of sense perception, but most likely in the intelligible area as well. That is, images which are not copies of the material world, as for instance, an image of justice, belong in the intelligible segment of the Divided Line.

---

[18] Ibid. p444-445.

Further, Jacob Klein argues that there is an important correspondence between the nature of an image and the nature of opinion: an image in the visible segment is special because it produces 'double-seeing', which refers to our ability, not to mistake an image for its original, but rather to see the original *through* the image[19] (114-115). In Klein's words an image is therefore "uniquely that which *is not* what it *is*"[20]. This is not the case with a visible object, which only is that which it is. An opinion also lies in between that which is (knowledge) and that which is not (ignorance). Hence it too occupies a sort of "double" status similar to that of the image of a concrete object. An opinion can be both ignorance and knowledge (477a-b) And just as a very poor image of an object is more false than a good one; so an opinion close to ignorance is more false than one closer to knowledge[21]. The essential point is that there are not simply images and opinions: but that there are bad, good, better, worse and best images and opinions[22]. In my view, it may be the case that Socrates focuses on the familiar relationship between a material objects and their images to explain and illustrate a more abstract relationship regarding the status of opinions. As an attack on the relativist and particularistic sophists, it is imperative for Socrates to show his interlocutors that not **all** opinions are the same; in much the same fashion as all images of an object are not of equal quality either.

But does this really matter? Even if one agrees that opinions and material images are of a similar status: this only illustrates just how deceptive and 'unreal' both of them are compared to **true** knowledge and its objects, the forms or the "originals". I do not deny this charge: it is true that Plato places the imagination in the same category as opinion and belief. However, I would argue that it is not explicitly clear that Socrates or any of his interlocutors reach true knowledge themselves[23]. And this is why the scale or range of opinions and images is so important. In the *Phaedrus* Socrates paints a striking image of

---

[19] Jacob Klein, A *Commentary on Plato's Meno* (North Carolina: The University of North Carolina Press) 1965, p114.
[20] Ibid, p115.
[21] It is of course possible that a "poor" image of a material object is not striving for life-like or material "likeness" and an artist of 'poor' images may rightly refuse to label these images false.
[22] In Book 3 Socrates says to Glaucon that: "Voluntary is the departure of the false belief from one who learns better, involuntary that of every true belief." (413a). We are thus unwilling to part with our true beliefs/opinions.
[23] J.J. Chambliss, *Imagination and reason in Plato, Aristotle, Vico, Rousseau, and Keats* (The Hague: Martinus Nijhoff), 1974, p11-12

the breathtaking journey of the winged deathless soul flying **outside** of the heavens: as it travels around and around "it beholds justice it self; it beholds moderation; it beholds knowledge"[24]. And Socrates says: "And this is the Gods life" (248a). As for the other non-divine souls there is only partial seeing often coupled with much confusion: many souls have their wings broken or maimed. Due to their partial seeing they have to "make use of opinion for nourishment" (248b). The life of beholding purely and constantly true knowledge is therefore not the fate for the human soul. Socrates often stresses that he does not have complete or certain knowledge: he makes assumptions and premises, he relies on trust and belief, and he cautions his interlocutors that if the assumption or premise they start from will prove to be wrong then they have to start all over again. This incessant revision of ideas is an essential part of doing philosophy.

In the *Meno* Socrates uses the image of Daedalus' statues to show how crucial it is to **ground** true beliefs because a true belief is *insecure* knowledge. But Meno does not understand what Socrates means:

Socrates: There's as little point in paying a lot of money for an unrestrained statue of his as there is for a runaway slave: it doesn't stay put. But Daedalus' pieces are so beautiful that they're worth a great deal if they're anchored…I mean this to an analogy for true beliefs. As long as they stay put, true beliefs too constitute a thing of beauty and do nothing but good. The problem is that they tend not to stay for long: they escape from the human soul and this reduces their value, unless they're anchored by working out the reason"97e-98a[25]

I follow Robin Waterfield in taking this key act of "working out the reason" to indicate that we need a chain of evidence or proof to make our beliefs more certain and more *like* knowledge[26]: true beliefs are *like* the very best images of stable knowledge. Also, Socrates is encouraging us to work out **why** we believe something: he is provoking us to

---

[24] Plato, *Phaedrus* trans, intro. by James H. Nichols Jr. (Ithaca: Cornell University Press) 1998. All following references from the *Phaedrus* will come from this translation and all numerical references are to the Stephanus pages.
[25] Plato, *Meno And Other Dialogues* trans. Robin Waterfield (New York: Oxford University Press) 2005, 97e-98a. All following references will come from this edition and translation by Waterfield and all numerical references are to the Stephanus pages.
[26] *Meno And Other Dialogues* Waterfield intro pp. xliii-xliv.

be *aware* of and question our opinions. Thus even if Plato never shows us the conversion of true beliefs into knowledge we are not to be dismayed or become cynical and grant all opinions equal value and status. We can and should still strive and search for knowledge and the best opinions.

To briefly summarize the above line of thought: one essential aspect of the discussion of images and opinions is that they are not all of equal value. And since Socrates indicates that there is bad, good and best opinion, one should trust that it is the same case with the imagination[27]. As I argued previously, the image-category in the divided line is partly used to illustrate the position and nature of opinions and thinking. However, images are more than illustrative props for opinions: Murray Wright Bundy argues that images and opinions are connected because they are both "versions" of knowledge and the original (Knowledge + Original vs. Opinions + Images): i.e. if our opinions are false then we will also construct false images[28]. I will discuss this further when turning to Socrates charge against poetry in Book 10. At this point I would like to stress that, *muthos* and *logos*, reason and imagination, are **both** put to use in the striving for more stable or "anchored" opinions.

To conclude, the image of the divided line on my reading attempts to illustrate **how** we think. It is a psychological and practical image, rather than a specific metaphysics or "Theory of Ideas". The divided line, like the image of the soul in the *Phaedrus*, is a myth or a metaphor. However, this does not mean that I for instance deny the meaning of ascent or descent: it only means that I do not view the divided line as a specific or literal formula for reaching the universals or the forms. Instead I agree with John Herman Randall, who argues that Plato gives us, not a fixed theory of ideas or knowledge, but rather a **vision** (*theoria*) of what is worth knowing. On this interpretation the ideas/forms do not reside in a separate or remote realm.[29] On this, less literal yet more direct and straight-forward approach, one may argue that we find the ideas *in the dialogues*, in logos

---

[27] *Republic* Bloom 462, footnote 5.
[28] Murray Wright Bundy, *The theory of Imagination in Classical and Mediaeval Thought* (University of Illinois studies in language and literature) vol. 12, no. 2-3, 1927, p48.
[29] John Herman Randall Jr. *Plato Dramatist of the Life of Reason* (New York: Columbia University Press) 1970, p195.

and discussion, not in some remote realm or state of mind. And we *access* the Ideas by talking and discussing[30]. This is important because rather than turning away from the world in image-less contemplation, we are to try to strive to perfect life here and now.

---

[30] Ibid, p197.

III. Images in Education and Poetry

Education and Poetry

The following section will discuss images, and image-making in relation to education and poetry[31]. Education and poetry were particularly close in ancient Greece. Theatre-going was a significant part of civic education and the theatre therefore was not simply a place one went to be entertained; it was also a place where one expected to learn.[32] Poetry thus occupied a "higher" status in Athens than it perhaps does nowadays. The present connection between poetry and education also rests on my proposal that Plato does not exclude or ban **all** poetry from education or philosophy. A central aim in the following discussion is therefore to show how **good** images can be of educational value, not only in the education of children, but also in philosophic discussion.

I will begin by addressing the nature of bad images and bad uses of images. As proposed previously, Plato is not in favour of *all* images and image-making, without qualification. Some images are not beneficial at all, but rather quite useless or worse, harmful. Bad images provoke the human tendency to emotional excess by displaying and encouraging, for instance over- indulgent lamenting, and wailing. Images can also be bad because they are not suitable for a specific audience. Finally, images unaccompanied by logos and by rational argumentation are not useful either. The sole purpose of images in philosophic discussion is **not** to simply dazzle and mesmerize. Rather, images, even though they might be alluring and beautiful, must also be grounded in *logos*.

Third, I will discuss good images and good **uses** of images. I will propose that Plato holds fantastical or outlandish images to be of more use than "realistic" or naturalistic ones because they challenge us to question our opinions and beliefs. This discussion must also address Book 10 of the *Republic*, with its legendary banning of the poets and promotion of heavy-handed state censorship. How does this square with my argument that Plato

---

[31] Please note that I use poetry in its widest meaning, referring to all the arts, including music, painting, theatre etc; and sometimes the terms poetry/art are used interchangeably.
[32] As Stephen Halliwell points out, it is important to keep poetry's "normative or paradigmatic status" in Athens in mind when we read Plato's critique of poetry, see *The Aesthetics of Mimesis* (Princeton: Princeton University Press) 2002, p75.

encourages poetry in philosophy? Another central aspect of a good image is that it **remains** an image, that is, that we keep in mind that it is not "reality". Only by seeing *through* an image can it be truly useful to philosophy. Images in philosophy are not just there to please our senses or our fancy; they are there to serve a purpose. In Plato's texts more elaborate images and myths are often introduced to change the 'tone' of a discussion, or to engage us emotionally and *impress* a point upon us.

As a final point, I will conclude this section with a brief explanation of why the image of Socrates as a stinging gadfly, or a torpedo fish, is a **good** image. To be stung by Socrates into doing philosophy is a compelling image of the nature of beneficial philosophical education, and this image also tells us something important about the task and the *place* of the philosopher.

Children's Images and Play

In Book 2 Socrates says that tales about gods doing horrific things to each other are not good for children (377e-378a). Primarily they are not good because children are not capable of grasping any "hidden sense" (378d) in a tale. In other words, feeding children with graphic images of the wild escapades of the gods is not beneficial because children are not able to judge or think metaphorically, to the same extent as adults. Telling children tales that focus on the excessive, outrageous, frightful and immoral behaviour of the gods set horrible examples for children, from *the point of view* of justice. In this respect, the gods are rotten role models, and a child reared on these tales will not think that doing something wrong is bad because he or she would after all "be doing only what the first and the greatest of the gods did" (378b). Indeed, Socrates indicates that "not even if [these tales] were true would I suppose they should so easily be told to thoughtless young things" (378a). In other words: even if we knew that the gods *did* behave in this manner, we should not tell our children this so carelessly.

Instead, tales should be adapted or specifically tailored to children (377b). In their musical education children should be told speeches, both true and false, and they are to begin with the false ones (376e). It is not always clear if Plato means lies or fictions when he speaks of the "false" (pseudos) tales because he uses the word *pseudos* to refer to **both** lies and fictions. This makes it tricky in determining if he is accusing the poets, in Book 2, of deceiving children deliberately (i.e. by lying) with their tales, or if they tell the wrong types of stories or fictions because they are deceived in their own perceptions of reality. Regardless, I tend to think that Plato is primarily concerned with the poets not adjusting their tales to the specific needs and abilities of children, with the result that children believe that gods actually behave in this fashion. Children do not understand the metaphorical character of the poetic depictions of the gods. Similarly, tales aimed at scaring children (381e) are not good either because they make "the children more cowardly" (381e). On this reading, from the point of view of **justice** and the teaching of justice to children, there is a need for *adequate* children's stories. The answer is not to cut out **all** tales and simply begin with empirical truths or facts. The footage on the evening news may be empirically true, but it is nevertheless too upsetting for a child to watch.

On the whole Socrates' and Adeimantus' discussion of children's tales in Book 2 strikes me as very "modern" and akin to our notions of child psychology. We often think that it is appropriate to prevent children from hearing and seeing certain things. Indeed, parents who let their children watch any type of entertainment and play any type of game tend to be seen as irresponsible or ignorant, or both. These adults do not have sufficient *knowledge*, or care or interest, in how children are different from adults. Ultimately, the health of the child's soul is what is at stake and Athenian mothers educating their young with these 'adult' type stories about the gods are not wise parents, just as parents today who take very young children to watch horror films or allow them to play violent computer games also are not **good** to their children. Thus, on a very basic and common sense level, there are certain images that are not suited for children, and this is why we tell them false tales (fictions) with some grains of truth in them (377a). As Socrates remarks, children are easily influenced or "plastic" (377b) and what one is told and taught in childhood tends to leave a *lasting* dent or impression on one's soul. Images for children that have not been tailored with this in mind are therefore bad.

False speeches in the form of tales and fictions are sometimes required for adults too. This is not, however, simply a matter of condescension or superiority, as when only the rulers in the city in speech are permitted to craft "noble" lies (414d) to trick the ignorant lower classes. Tales are also used to refer to our distant past, and we tell these tales, says Socrates, because "we don't know where the truth about ancient things lies – likening the lie to the truth as best we can, don't we also make it useful?" (382d) That is, we do not have full nor first-hand knowledge of the very distant past, and therefore we have to rely on tales to make sense of what we believe to be the closest to what *actually* happened. Of course it is crucial to remember that these accounts of our past are tales and fictions, and not first-hand reporting. The classification of good and bad images, even with regards to adults, does not solely map onto the categories of empirically true and false. Images are also judged by ethical criteria: Are they good for us? Are they bad? As Socrates remarks in Book 1, sometimes it is better to withhold the empirical truth from a friend who is insane or drunk (332a) because it will not be *good* for him or her to hear it.

Finally, with regards to education, Socrates stresses the importance not only of the types of images told to children but also **how** they are to learn: "don't use force in training the children in the studies, but rather play" (537a). As with tales, play is not *only* for children. After having spoken quite passionately about who should, and who should not be allowed to learn dialectics Socrates remarks: "But I seem to have been somewhat ridiculously affected just now…I forgot that we were playing and spoke rather intensely"(536b-c). The city in speech is a product of this play, it is make-believe and pretending and no matter how splendid: it is "only" an image'. Image-making is the use of play *in discussion*. Crafting images in speech allows for playful, free testing of ideas, opinions and assumptions. Potentially, it can also illustrate the broader implications of a specific idea or value, such as justice. The city in speech teaches us about justice through an image; it materializes and brings an abstract invisible idea to life. Perfect justice may sound alluring, but imagining how a perfectly just city would actually come into being and maintain itself allows us to "see" that it might also have some unjust consequences. The playful aspect of philosophy, through image-making and pretending, allows us to **see** and elaborate on an idea together in discussion.

The Tyrant

Make-believe and pretending is thus beneficial in both children's' education and in philosophic discussion. But there **are** limits: it is not good to pretend to be a truly mad (396a) or 'incurable' soul. In Book 9, when the time has come to craft the tyrannical man, Socrates and his interlocutors do **not** pretend to be tyrants like they earlier pretended to be founders (577b). Instead they pretend to be judges who can question someone who has lived close to the tyrant, someone who is able "with his thought to creep into a man's disposition and see through it – a man who is not like a child looking from outside and overwhelmed by the tyrannic pomp" (577a). This person has seen through the façade of the tyrant and has caught a glimpse of his soul. The questioning of this person reveals that the tyrant is least of all free and happy: "Throughout his entire life he is full of fear, overflowing with convulsions and pains" (579e). Ultimately the tyrant's world is marked by loneliness and complete ignorance of both freedom and friendship (576a). It is harmful for the soul to pretend to be such a person. But this does not mean that he cannot be discussed. To adequately *judge* the tyrant's soul one must be able to see through his façade (577a), otherwise it might dazzle one into believing that his life is wonderful: crowded with praise, license and a whimsical ability to satisfy his every sensual desire. Only by seeing through the tyrant's exterior image, can one judge his soul and **see** that one ought not to live the way he does. This is not a good soul or a good life. It is a life purged of moderation, ruled by a soul stung into a mad frenzy (573b).

Images in Logos

An image's usefulness also depends on what it is framed by. Images *unaccompanied* by questions and criticism are not useful. If rhetoric can be said to be "the art of making long speeches without being questioned"[33], images in philosophy belong **in discussion**. The mode of discussion will "corner" images with questions and criticisms. Further, images are not a goal in themselves in discussion. Instead, one central component in useful philosophic discussion is truthfulness and a sincere willingness to adhere to this "rule". If one **only** goes into a discussion with the aim of "winning", no matter what, and one is prepared to be untruthful and insincere in order to win, then the search and collective

---

[33] The *Republic*, Bloom Interpretative Essay, p326.

striving for better ethical opinions is much more difficult[34]. Images need therefore to confirm to this promise of truthfulness and we should not carelessly construct images in speech with the sole aim to win an argument.

Another problem with images in speech arises when it is not **pointed out** that images are images, and not empirical facts or ethical absolutes. A skilled sophist can manipulate his audience with *selectively* chosen images, often taken out of context from the works of the great poets, and make them appear as if they convey the whole truth about empirical and normative matters[35]. This is at the very heart of Socrates' charge against the sophists; they are only concerned with that which **appears** probable, and that which will win an argument; they have turned away from any deep concern for the true and the false. In Plato's words, they are preoccupied with seeming rather than being (596e). In contrast, Socrates for instance emphasizes that he can only give us an **image** of the idea of the good (506e). And the image is only an imperfect copy of the true idea.

A person educated by sophists can produce strikingly beautiful images in speech, yet below their appealing surface these images are often empty of insight or truth. In the *Symposium*, Agathon's image of the god Eros is lovely yet heavy with exaggeration and ornament: "love who showers benignity over the world, and before whose presence all harsh passions flee and perish; the author of all soft affections…the father of grace, and delicacy, and gentleness, and delight and persuasion, and desire" (197d) .This praise of Eros, this elaborate image, certainly *sounds* beautiful and when Agathon is finished "a loud murmur of applause arose from all present, so becomingly had the fair youth spoken" (197e). Yet upon reflection one wonders what it **means**? In Agathon's image Eros in the end is *everything*, yet that is not what he initially seeks to argue. Socrates, albeit with *false* modesty, points out: "I, in my simplicity, imagined that the truth ought to be spoken, concerning each of the topics of our praise" (198d). Agathon's image is only

---

[34] Peterman, *On Plato* 2000, p47.
[35] It should be noted that Socrates can also be charged with selectively picking from the poets and quoting them unfairly or out of context. In my view this illustrates Plato's difficult task of distinguishing the philosopher from the sophist.

concerned with laying on as much praise as possible in the honour of Eros, regardless of whether it conforms with his initial premise, or if it actually applies to the God or not.

Furthermore, Agathon's speech also represents a shallow and deficient use of myth and allegory. Even though he is critical enough to employ myths selectively and include some independent reasoning, rather than simply repeating what he has memorized from the poets, there are logical problems[36]. For instance: Agathon uses *ate*[37] as an allegory for Eros; yet *ate* causes both good and bad things, which goes against what Agathon is seeking to argue, namely that Eros is only good and fair. Logical problems are however, not glaring; rather they are veiled and glossed over by the beauty of the image as a whole. Therefore, chances are that without Socrates present, the speech would have been accepted without mention by the others. The main point at stake in the present context is that images skillfully crafted and convincingly presented **can** be bad, especially if the speaker's intention is like Thrasymachus', in Book 1 to just go away "like a bathman" after delivering his speech[38]. Notably, Agathon does not go away but stays and is both open and graceful to Socrates critique and questions[39]. His intentions are not to deliberately deceive, yet his speech "barely conceals the arbitrary playfulness of an imagination grounded in little else than ornamentation and its own preferences"[40].

Images, to be useful, therefore need to be grounded *within* logos: images unaccompanied by rational argumentation are not useful because they run the risk of both deceiving and acquiring, so to speak, a life of their own, freed from purpose and value. To be of use to

---

[36] Kevin Corrigan and Elena Glazov-Corrigan *Plato's Dialectic at Play: Argument Structure and Myth in the Symposium* (University Park, Pennsylvania: The Pennsylvania State University Press) 2004, p87-88.
[37] Ate was "the Greek personification of infatuation, the rash foolishness of blind impulse, usually caused by guilt and leading to retribution. The goddess of discord and mischief, she tempted man to do evil, and then lead him to ruin. Ate is regarded as the daughter of Zeus and Eris, the goddess of strife. "Ate." *Encyclopedia Mythica* from Encyclopedia Mythica Online:
http://www.pantheon.org/articles/a/ate.html.
[38] This danger is similar to Plato's concern with writing; see especially his discussion in the *Phaedrus*: while writing does not necessarily "go away" like the sophist, it does not answer back or change either. Writing therefore also runs the risk of being a deceptive image, and if we do not see through it we are not being critical enough.
[39] Thrasymachus does not go away either, and he does present more specific definitions of justice. The issue at stake is that Socrates says that **he had in mind** to go away "like a bathman', but the discussion in the *Republic* changes this.
[40] Corrigan and Glazov, *Plato's Dialectic*, 2004 p89.

philosophic discussion, images **must** exist alongside questions and criticisms, or they will become "unanchored" and take off like one of Daedalus' beautiful statues in the *Meno* (97e). Agathon's image of Eros, however beautiful, can be criticised for being frivolously pursued for its own sake. Yet it is "reined" in by Socrates, who questions Agathon, and Agathon is willing and open to engage in a revision of his image.

Bad Images: Tragedy and Human Agency

In Book 3, Adeimantus and Socrates cut out the wailing and lamenting in poetic depictions of heroes and Gods (387d). If the young hear these types of tales they too will become weak. The way Homer presents Achilles is not to their liking: his actions are not befitting of a great hero and son of a goddess (388a-b). However, the greatest criticism of poetry in general and tragedy in particular, comes in Book 10. The tragedian, who depicts characters in extreme sorrow and misfortune wallowing in severe emotions, is a dealer of bad images, not because sorrow or grief is so bad; rather it is the *over-indulgence* and incessant focusing on the tragic aspects of life in an unhealthy and obsessive fashion that Plato attacks (605b). Thus it is not necessarily that tragic poets are all depicting empirical falsities; but their images are biased in the sense that they *deliberately* focus on the weak part in the human soul, the part which longs to give up and lose itself in endless grief; the part which shamelessly and vulgarly laments and wails without restraint. These images are harmful psychologically because they feed the part of our soul which takes pleasure in crude imitation, exaggeration, and in hopelessness (605b). In other words, tragedy focuses on that which is lower or baser in the soul, without clearly indicating this. The tragic poet, says Socrates, makes "things that are ordinary by the standard of truth" (605a). This poet does not adequately portray that which is **not** ordinary or "low" in the soul. And if we nourish and educate our souls only on tragedies we consequently nurture a distorted part of the soul.

Thus, it is not that Plato rejects the world depicted by the tragic poets completely; that he does not somehow recognize the tragic aspects of human existence where, for example, the just get punished, prosecuted or killed while the unjust walk free or are celebrated as just when they are not. In the *Apology*, and *Phaedo* he does indeed portray just that: the trial and execution of Socrates, a just man. But, the difference is **how** Plato portrays the reaction to tragic events. We do not see Socrates going mad or giving in to uncontrollable grief at the news of his pending death sentence. Instead we see a very calm, collected and reasonable Socrates, even in facing severe personal injustice. In the end the tragic poets and Plato are both guilty of deliberately choosing to focus on specific aspects of human existence: one on the fateful, deterministic aspects where one is set on giving up and losing oneself in sorrow and darkness; the other on the fact that there is human agency; we **can** choose how we respond to horrific events, and for the health of the soul we are better to move on and heal ourselves *as quickly as we can* (604c-d).

On the whole, I think that Plato takes issue with a civic education based solely on tragedy, not because there is absolutely nothing to learn from tragedies, but because tragedy fails to disclose the idea of **striving** to make oneself as good as is humanly possible (613a-b). The constant search and striving for human betterment and for knowledge (490b) can be said to be one thing which sets philosophy apart from tragedy. In the *Meno* Socrates says that even though he would not necessarily support every single aspect of their preceding argument: "there's one proposition that I'd defend to the death, if I could, by argument and by action: that as long as we think we should search for what we don't know we'll be better people – less fainthearted and less lazy – than if we were to think that we had no chance of discovering what we don't know and that there's no point in even searching for it"(86b-c). This is mostly **not** what tragedies teach or inspire us to believe. Indeed, some tragic depictions may inspire not to better ourselves since it does not matter at all what we do, either in this life or after we die.

So what can tragedies teach us? How can they be of use to philosophy? If we display strong emotions when certain things in life happen to us; this indicates what it is in human life that is worth living for and focusing on[41]. In other words, the *causes* of grief in tragedies depict real and important things in life: if the loss of a close friend or child causes grief, it indicates that family and friendship are crucial *goods* in human life. And Socrates does *not deny* grief in Book 10. He denies wallowing in it, or becoming mad as

---

[41] Halliwell, *The Aesthetics of Mimesis*, 2002 p107.

a result of it: "rather one must always habituate the soul to turn as quickly as possible to curing and setting aright what has fallen and is sick" (604c-d)

But does watching a tragedy make us want to behave in this way? We do not necessarily want to copy all poetic depictions. On this charge, Plato is being inflexible and too worried about the influence of poetry on the soul. And, more importantly, if tragedies, with their stress on the excessive and extreme, are not the ultimate form of civic education, as Socrates and Adeimantus seem to suggest, how balanced is it to proceed to cut out almost **all** imitative drama? Yet even in this rather harsh moment Socrates reminds Adeimantus that their argument is not set in stone: "We must be persuaded by it until someone persuades us with another and finer one" (388e). And, again in Book 10 he tells Glaucon: "if poetry directed to pleasure and imitation have any argument to give showing that they should be in a city with good laws, we should be delighted to receive them back from exile, since we are aware that we ourselves are charmed by them" (607c). Plato **invites** the poets to take up his challenge and refute him: in other words, they are to show us how their poetry is beneficial. The complete banning and censoring of the poets in Book 10 may be part of this very deliberate provocation: Plato wants the poets to answer for themselves, and give an account of how their creations are good.

Moreover, it is important to keep the **significance** of the poets in mind: as civic educators and not just entertainers. Plato puts the standing of the poets as the indisputable educators of their day into question, and he invites us to ask: Why should we accept what the poets say uncritically? Why should we agree with their depiction of reality? Socrates therefore often stresses that poets' tales are not **the** truth: and we can choose not to believe them or take them seriously (608a). If the poets enjoy the status of official spokespersons of the gods, not to be questioned, then their images have become separated from logos and criticism. But if images in poetry are a vehicle for discussion, debate and criticism then they can have an important function and value. The politically dangerous image-maker is thus the person who claims to 'report' straight from god to a docile audience which does not question his claims.

Nevertheless, I willingly admit that Book 10 is strange: Book 3 and 4 allowed for some limited imitation, and some poets in the city in speech. Suddenly, in Book 10 **all** poetry, except for hymns to the gods and the celebrations of good men (607a), is banned. And why does Socrates, after having trashed and banned poetry, **end** book 10 with a myth of his own?[42] Even if Plato wants to provoke and question the poets and their claim to authoritative status: why does he do it in this fashion? Book 10 can be read and interpreted on many different levels: my tentative discussion does not achieve any final, neat or smooth interpretation which ties up all the discrepancies and contradictions. It can only touch upon a few of the layers of meaning in the text. On my reading, the *Republic* as a whole is a brilliant image of philosophic discussion. Part of its brilliance is that it refuses to be tied or nailed down to any final interpretation.

The remainder of my discussion of Book 10 will center on the distinction between the good and the bad, in poetry and education. Plato does not only distinguish between poets and philosophers; he also distinguishes between the good and the bad. Therefore, a bad artist is related to a sophist or a bad thinker; and there is kinship between a good poet and a philosopher: In Murray Wright Bundy's words "just as the true artist and true philosopher were one for Plato…so the false artist and false thinker came under the same condemnation. No thinker has ever established a closer relation between poetry and philosophy"[43]. And as Socrates indicates in Book 10, what is ultimately at stake is the "contest that concerns becoming good or bad" (608b). This contest is more important than deciding if someone is a poet or a philosopher.

Socrates' claim that the artist (here meaning all artists) lacks real knowledge and can't judge if his imitation is good or bad (602a) is puzzling: for instance, it contradicts the *Symposium*, where it is indicated that the poet will, at least potentially, bring forth

---

[42] David Roochnik, *Beautiful City: The Dialectical Character of Plato's Republic* (Ithaca, New York: Cornell University Press) 2003, p121.
[43] Bundy, *Theory of Imagination* 19p40. Also compare Percy Bysshe Shelley "Defence of Poetry" in *The Four Ages of Poetry* ed. H.F.B Brett-Smith (Oxford: Basil Blackwell) 1953 : "The distinction between poets and prose writers is a vulgar error, [as is] the distinction between philosophers and poets, Plato was essentially a poet – the truth and splendour of his imagery and the melody of his language is the most intense that is possible to conceive"p29.

intelligence and "every other power of the mind"(209b)[44]. Bundy argues that Plato is not just rejecting **all** art and poetry: rather he recognizes that "an adequate philosophy must explain the activity of the artists rather than deny the reality of their products"[45]. So, in Book 10 of the *Republic*, Plato attacks the *specific* notion of the artist who depicts the world as he sees it. *This* artist is on the same level as the sophist; he is never capable of grasping a world beyond particular impressions[46]. In other words, Plato attacks **both** bad artists and bad thinkers: and he is highly critical of the idea that art is **objective** because it imitates the actual world. This art tends toward materialism and lacks the notion that that which is being imitated is also the expression of something ideal or ethical**.**

This type of art is also linked to **relativity**: we are all entitled to copy or imitate what we see around us *as we see it* in the same fashion as everyone is entitled to an opinion, none better than the other**,** which makes each the author of his own wisdom (561c). Everyone is then as a result, relative to himself, right, which effectively creates a world that **cancels out** the need for discussing and refuting and revising ideas and opinions[47]. The principal charges against bad poets and thinkers are thus that their objects (their art and their speeches) create false objectivity or total relativity where there is no ranking, criticizing or revision of opinions and beliefs.

The recurring image of the painter in Book 10, holding up a mirror to nature (596d) "objectively" copying what he sees can thus be interpreted in different ways. First, it reads as a metaphor and critique of poets who claim the status of spokespersons of the Gods (598e), merely "copying" out the deeds and thoughts of the Gods. This act of "transparency" is dangerous because it makes it seem as if the artist is not *doing* anything, that he is not presenting a very specific viewpoint. Secondly, the mirror-image

---

[44] Plato, *The Symposium of Plato: The Shelley Translation* ed. and intro. by David O'Connor (South Bend, Indiana: St. Augustine's Press) 2002. All following references from the *Symposium* will come from this translation and all numerical references are to the Stephanus pages. In the *Symposium*, Socrates reports that Diotima told him that those who are "pregnant" in body are attracted to the opposite sex, "but they whose souls are far more pregnant than their bodies, conceive and produce that which is more suitable to the soul. What is suitable to the soul? Intelligence, and every other power and excellence of the mind, of which all poets, and all other artists who are creative and inventive, are the authors" 209b, p54.
[45] Bundy, *Theory of Imagination* 1927 p31.
[46] Ibid., p32.
[47] Bundy, *Theory of Imagination*, 1927 p33.

also reads as an attack on the sophist who disguises opinions as facts. Like the naturalistic painter giving us only what he "sees", so the sophist, with his clever use of that which *seems* believable to his audience, strikes them as stating objective facts[48]. This acceptance is just as dangerous as complete relativity because it also removes the need for inquiry. On both readings the mirror-image relieves the poet and sophist from responsibility for their creations, and in both cases they are, so to speak, hiding behind them. Yet they do have a stake in how their creations or their images are received: status, money, and fame, to name only a few rewards, hang in the balance. One should be aware of the self-serving aspect of their work; in other words, we should remember **who** is making poetry and speeches.

Good Images

I now want to show how Plato's critique of holding a 'mirror up to nature" helps us understand why fantastical and outlandish or strange images as more useful than realistic or materialist ones. First, fantastical images span *further* into new realities beyond the material world, and highlight that there is another world apart from the one we perceive with our senses, in very much the opposite fashion of the artist holding up a mirror to nature[49]. Instead of copying the familiar around us, the fantastical images expand our world in an attempt at capturing the immaterial, spiritual or ethical, reminding us not to see the sensible and material as somehow more real than the abstract or invisible. In support of this view I turn once again to the images in the *Republic*.

The Cave does not depict a concrete, familiar reality. As Glaucon remarks, "it's a strange image.....and strange prisoners you're telling of". And Socrates replies: "They're like us" (515a). The prisoners are **like** us but they are not us: Socrates reminds us that the Cave *remains* an image. He makes use of the image to illustrate the education of the soul, one of the most important questions for philosophy. To employ an elaborate image at this

---

[48] At the beginning of Book 10 when Socrates speaks of artistic imitation, and how this artist can make every kind of object of the artisans, Glaucon says: "That's quite a wonderful sophist you speak of" (595d).
[49] I am not, however, trying to suggest that this material art cannot tell us important things about our world by for instance exposing misery, inequality, suffering etc. But Plato's images mostly do not do this.

point indicates a decisive connection between images and ideas **in speech**. Or, as Roochnik puts it, we see that philosophy cannot do without poetry or myth[50]. With poetic association, metaphor and a vivid, rich and imaginative language we **do** get a glimpse of another reality: a striking materialization of the state of the human soul in its want of education and knowledge, expressing also our longing for making the abstract and the invisible more concrete and visible. The Cave, the myth of Er, the image of the soul's journey in the *Phaedrus*, and other strange and unforgettable images in Plato's texts illustrate "correct" poetry: and reveals how indispensable it *can* be to philosophy, especially in education and discussion.

Hence, Plato does not only confront poets to "justify" themselves, nor does he only criticise them: he produces poetry too. In so doing, he both challenges and pays poetry the ultimate compliment. By employing myth and fantastical images at critical points in the dialogues he **shows** us how indispensable images are, both to education and to philosophy[51]. Images are in the dialogues because they are an essential part of philosophic discussion, which simultaneously educates everyone, including the philosopher himself, about ethical truths. I do not think that Plato necessarily had to communicate in images. In my view, Plato could have done without myth had he chosen to; but his images are there because they do something specific i.e. they serve a purpose or have a function, that is *essential* to the text. The myths are not there for those who do not understand the other more "sophisticated" parts of the discussion. And they are not neat little summaries of the preceding discussion either. Rather, the images and myths are in the text to engage and impress us: either to give us hope and courage to go on searching for better opinions and more certain knowledge, or to capture the imagination in order to make us **see** that which we say or think, and to awaken the passion or eros for philosophy[52].

---

[50] Roochnik, *Beautiful City*, 2003 p114.
[51] Roochnik, *Beautiful City*, 2003 p111.
[52] Or in Percy Bysshe Shelley's beautiful formulation: "poetry strips the veil of familiarity from the world…it compels us to feel that which we perceive, and to imagine that which we know. It creates a new universe" "Defence of Poetry", p56 in *The Four Ages of Poetry* ed. H.F.B Brett-Smith (Oxford: Basil Blackwell) 1953.

An example of this type of imaginary seeing is the moulding of the unjust man's soul in speech, at the end of Book 9. This man is unjust but has a reputation of being just and Socrates suggests that in order to discuss with the person who says that this unjust man has the best of both worlds, they proceed by "moulding an image of the soul in speech so that the man who says these things will see just what he has been saying" (588b). Glaucon wonders what sort of image this might be, and Socrates replies "one of those natures such as the tales they say used to come into being in olden times –the Chimera, Scylla, Cerberus, and certain others" (588c). The multi-headed beast image helps Glaucon picture, in his mind's eye, the state of this man's soul: he gets to see how imbalanced his soul is, how enslaved, depraved and captivated it is by its lower, baser part. The state of the unjust man's soul is brought to life *through* the image. It makes the abstract (in this case the unjust soul which seems just) visible, and it is more effective than plainly stating: "the unjust man who seems just is enslaved to his baser passions therefore his life is not wonderful and happy". To me this exemplifies the proposition that images are an important part of philosophic discussion.

Stinging and Numbing Education for the Soul
I will wrap up this section by a brief discussion of the image of Socrates as a stinging gadfly, or numbing torpedo fish, as Meno calls him. Plato's shorter dialogues discuss one excellence or virtue, such as friendship or self-control, and they mostly end in *aporia* or perplexity. This perplexity, as Robin Waterfield points out, is very different from ignorance because the mental frustration it creates is the **awareness** of ignorance. To have a dialogue end in *aporia* is not the mark of failure; it is the beginning of philosophy. If we do not recognize that we need to revise our opinions and beliefs then we are not open to engage in philosophy. Therefore, to be trapped in self-contradiction by Socrates is beneficial for the soul[53].

In the *Meno* Socrates presses Meno to see that he does not know what excellence as a whole really *is* (79e). He cannot define it, and when pressured he gets annoyed and accuses Socrates of infecting him with bewilderment, and of casting debilitating spells on

---
[53] The *Meno*, Waterfield intro., p viii.

him. He retorts to insulting Socrates: "If you'll allow me a little joke, I think I know the perfect image for you: in appearance and all other respects you're just like one of those flat sea-fish, torpedoes. I mean, the torpedo numbs anyone who comes near enough to touch it, and I think you've done the same kind of thing to me" (80a). Socrates replies that he will only accept the numbing image if it implies that **he also** is numb from not knowing: "if the torpedo numbs other people by the fact it's numb itself, I am indeed like it, but otherwise I'm not. It's not that I make other people stuck while being clear myself; no, I make other people stuck by virtue of the fact that I am stuck myself" (80c)[54].

Socrates does not want to numb Meno so much that he takes offence and leaves. It is a fine balancing act that is required for their conversation to remain on friendly terms, but it is imperative that it does. Socrates wants Meno to think for himself, but after the torpedo insult, Socrates shifts his strategy and instead of focusing on Meno he offers him **a story** about the wisdom of the mystery cults[55]. Why? Peterman argues that the religious story is not there to further focus on Socrates' ideas "but to present neutral ideas and images, a territory where our ideas can be reworked outside the consequences of the real world, similar to play therapy with children"[56]. Socrates tailors the story to fit Meno's needs at the specific moment in the discussion. The myth shifts the **tone** and the focus of the discussion. Meno needs confidence to carry on with their search. He needs hope. Later on in the dialogue after the slave boy and geometry experiment has been carried out, Socrates has succeeded in showing Meno that being stuck and perplexed is good:
Socrates: The numbing did him good then?
Meno: I'd say so. (84c)

---

[54] Socrates willingly admits that which he does not know. By virtue of having put his ego and fear of ridicule aside he is "ahead' of others in discussion. He is not afraid of admitting what he does not know. However, this may not strike one as democratic enough: after all, how Meno learns is quite clear from the numbing incident, but exactly how Socrates learns is not. Yet I would argue that discussion is stimulating and important "even" for Socrates. For instance, in the *Republic* Socrates is actively **challenged** by his interlocutors who are unwilling to swallow just anything he tries to sneak past them. He also does not know exactly where the discussion will take them.
[55] Peterman, *On Plato,* 2000 p38.
[56] Ibid., p38-39.

In the *Apology* Socrates warns his fellow Athenians: "if you put me to death, you will not easily find another who, if I may use a ludicrous comparison, clings to the state as a sort of gadfly to a horse that is large and well-bred but rather sluggish because of its size, so that it needs to be aroused" (30 line34-36)[57]. Moments before offering them this image Socrates has told them that they should be grateful for what the God commanded him to do because he has spent his whole life persuading them to improve their souls. His stinging and arousing function has thus not been malicious or selfish, nor has it been carried out solely for its own frivolous sake. Socrates stings and perplexes those around him to get them to turn to care for the betterment and improvement of their souls (31 line14).

In my view, the stinging image is vital to philosophy. Firstly, it encourages those stung to start *thinking for themselves* rather than simply accepting that which they are told. To reformulate: it teaches us to question, to distinguish between better and worse and to be aware of the process of revision of ideas and beliefs. When Socrates stings us we realize that that which we thought was secure or stable knowledge was not so. Of course, if we do not go on to find a better replacement for the opinion we lost we may feel like Socrates came and 'robbed' us. To be stung can thus be upsetting for some. Secondly, the gadfly on the back of Athens suggests to me that a *good* philosopher does not turn away from the political. He does not withdraw in contemplation; he is not otherworldly. The proper role of the philosopher, like the Athenian democratic political citizen, is to question and criticize his fellow citizens. And as the following section will attempt to argue: it is only in a democracy that the philosopher may occupy this position.

---

[57] Plato, *Euthyphro, Apology, Crito* trans. F.J. Church (New York: Macmillan Publishing Company) 1948 line 34-36, p37. All following references from the Apology are from this translation and all numerical references are to the Stephanus pages.

IV. Images: Democracy and the Ideal
Ideal and Democracy

The final section of this paper will consider images, and image-making in connection with the ideal and democracy. The discussion of the ideal will center on the proposal that the ideal is effectively expressed **through** images: in the *Republic* one ideal is the city in speech; another one is the idea of the Good, illustrated by the image of the Sun. I will argue that the just city, both as a political program, and as an analogy of the best soul, ultimately falls apart, and dies. But this is not a failure. On my reading it ties into philosophy's need for criticism: ideas come into being, live, die and are revised continually[58]. Philosophy, by means of criticism, *needs* democracy. It is in the democratic space, out of diversity, tolerance, freedom of speech, and frank speech[59], that new ideas are more likely to be born, and once in existence, are more likely to be criticised and revised.

This, however, is not to suggest that democracy is also not being criticized in the *Republic*; quite the contrary. Yet, I do not believe that democracy in the end is desirable in the *Republic* **only** because the city in speech is not possible in reality[60]. This would make it a meagre substitute. On my reading, the *spirit* of questioning and criticism vital to philosophy is more likely to exist in a democracy, whereas it does not appear to exist at all in the city in speech. In addition, democracy **also** needs philosophy. It needs it in order to not lapse into relativity and false speech. It needs it to not become self-righteous, lazy or excessive. This is as applicable and important in our liberal democracies as it was in 5th century Athens. The philosopher may not be the politician but he/she does have an important place in a democracy. In the end my argument seeks to stress the connections, not only between images and the ideal, on the one hand, and between images and democracy on the other. It also seeks to illustrate that there is a *connection* between the

---

[58] I here follow Peterman who illustrates the importance of death, life and reincarnation to philosophy, see *On Plato*, 2000 pp34-56.
[59] Sara S. Monoson, Plato's *Democratic Entanglements* (Princeton, New Jersey: Princeton University Press) 2000 *Parrhesia* is defined as the cultural practice of frank speech or truthful political criticism in Athens, p176.
[60] Patrick J. Deneen, *Democratic Faith* (Princeton, New Jersey: Princeton University Press) 2005, p199.

ideal and democracy, and more generally between philosophy and democracy[61]. Images and image-making are important aspects of both the ideal and democracy, as they relate to discussion and philosophy.

I will begin to develop the connection between images and the ideal by examining the city in speech, the idea of the Good, and the idea of the good life. Second, with regards to democracy, I will turn once more to the collective nature of image-making in the *Republic*, and the importance more generally of the death, life and reincarnation of ideas, to philosophy. While staying focused on the *Republic*, this discussion will also draw on images from the *Symposium* and *Meno*. I end by suggesting that democracy provides the space for philosophy to criticise and question, and philosophy helps to keep democracy from deteriorating.

City in speech: the Just City
I now turn to the image Socrates and his interlocutors create in the *Republic*: a just city with philosopher-kings (472c-d), communal sex and love (457c-d), and bans on poetry (397d-e), and innovation (424b). A city where everyone performs his or her designated function: a *truly* functional, super-organized, efficient city. Did Plato really want us to live in a city like this? Did Socrates, who seeks out novelty[62], and who blends myth and poetry into his speech, want to live there? Would he be allowed? So many of the things that are banned in the just city are at the same time employed by its very creators: again, we are left to wonder what we are to do with all the discrepancies between what is said can be done in their just city, and what the founders say and do themselves. Also, if the city in speech is **the** ultimate ideal do we really want it in any shape or form?

---

[61] Please note that with the ideal I do not simply mean for instance, the impossible or the fanatic; nor do I use democracy to specifically refer to one person- one vote. As my discussion progresses I hope it will become clear what I mean by both the ideal and democracy. For now, suffice it to say that the ideal even though it can be extreme, generally refers to the very best or the "highest, while with democracy I primarily speak of the democratic cultural practices and the **space** democracy creates, rather than strict equality and the act of voting.

[62] In the opening of the *Republic*, Socrates is on his way down to the Piraeus (outside the city walls) to watch a foreign festival.

But the city in speech begins to crumble at the beginning of Book 5 where Polemarchus makes Socrates revisit and re-formulate his previous statements about love, sex and family in the city. Socrates counters with the three wave image (457b) and the discussion goes into soaring heights culminating in the idea of the Good, the Line and the Cave in Books 5 through 7: all brilliant and strange images. Yet are we convinced that love is ever adequately incorporated into the just city? David Roochnik argues that the city falls apart (i.e. becomes an actual impossibility) *precisely* because it fails to incorporate eros. Instead it tries to suppress it. And since eros is a prerequisite for anyone who seeks to do philosophy, philosophy itself cannot exist in the city[63]. Unfortunately it is not within the scope of this project to discuss the central role of eros in more detail. For my purposes, the main point is that the passion and *space* for collective image-making required for philosophy and discussion appears to be glaringly absent in the city in speech.

After Polemarchus' demand for a more thorough treatment of eros it is Glaucon's turn. He interrupts Socrates' description of the prescribed behaviour of the guardians: "Is it possible for this regime to come into being, and how is it ever possible?"(471c). Socrates defends their image by pointing out that it can still be good even if it is *not* practically possible (472d). Notably he takes the painter as one example: if he paints a human being more beautiful than anyone has actually seen, then this image is not any less good than a more realistic portrait. (472e). He also cautions Glaucon about the difference between speech and deed, "Can anything be done as it is said?" (473a): this is an important aspect of the proper function of the ideal. We are not of sound mind if we imagine that we can install a specific ideal completely in actuality. To believe this is to forget that the ideal, this image in speech, has to **remain** an image to be truly useful. This does not, however, mean that we should not try to change things: only that we should be aware of the difference between speech and deed and that we should remember that in "real" life we need to accommodate the demands of *more* than one specific ideal.

---

[63] Roochnik, *Beautiful City* 2003 p58.

Glaucon appears satisfied with Socrates' defence of their city for the time being. But at the end of Book 9, after the philosopher kings have been introduced and the education of the soul has been described, Glaucon again revisits the possibility of their city:

Glaucon: "You mean he will [mind the political things] in the city whose foundation we have now gone through, the one that has its place in speeches, since I don't suppose it exists anywhere on earth"

Socrates: "But in heaven" I said, "perhaps, a pattern is laid up for the man who wants to see and found a city within himself on the basis of what he sees. It doesn't make any difference whether it is or will be somewhere. For he would mind the things of this city alone, and of no other" (592a-b).

If the city in speech is not an actual political program, how are we to understand it? One interpretation is that the initial and only topic of concern, the only **real** object of their search for justice, is the soul[64]. The city thus only serves as a magnifying glass for the soul, ultimately prescribing how we are to model and order our souls to become truly just, regardless of which regime we happen to live under (492a) On this reading the city in speech is *an image* of the soul and its different parts. In the just soul the reasoned part, with help from the spirited, masters and keeps the appetitive part under control (441d). Socrates comment about the city in heaven does attests to this, yet recall that in this sentence Socrates also says: "*perhaps*, a pattern is laid up for the man who wants to see and found a city within himself"(592b, my emphasis). Socrates does not claim this to be certain. Nor does he tell Glaucon that this is what he should do, even though he might believe that erotic Glaucon is in need of some self-mastering and proper ordering of his soul. Is the city in speech then an ideal blueprint for the soul; and if so, is the just soul any **more** possible than the just city?

While I believe that much of the discussion is indeed about the soul and its relation to justice, I do not think that the city/soul analogy is without tensions. John Deneen offers a useful interpretation: the city/soul analogy does not fit seamlessly because the *structure*

---

[64] At the beginning, they *only* search for justice in the city because it is bigger than the soul, 368e.

of the just city does not need its entire population to have just ordered souls: instead justice is dependent on the specific relations between the different classes in the city (432a). Only the guardians have just souls in the just city, no one else[65]. Justice is thus only achieved by a forceful suppression of the desiring appetitive souls. If the city in speech, with the guardians in charge, actually represents the soul, then **each** human soul has to govern over its lower parts, with the aid of, for example, the myth of the metals (415a), which on this reading would be a story one part of the soul, tells another part. Somehow this approach seems impossible: even though the soul may indeed be made up of various parts, with the reasoning part presiding over the others in a just soul, the different parts of the soul are still *conscious* of each other. In other words, is it possible to tell one's lower self a noble lie? From this viewpoint the actualization of the perfectly just soul also appears impossible.

However, the overall *connection* between the city and soul still stands and the city in speech is political *even* in illustrating the soul: if politics can be said to be linked to psychology through the city/soul analogy, so can the concerns of the soul also be said to be political. On my reading, Plato firmly links the two: if we do not try to know and better our souls, we cannot expect to know or improve the political. However, it could be objected that Socrates' remarks about both the "pattern laid out in heaven" (592a), and the philosopher leading a private life hiding "under a little wall" (496d), are not encouraging from a political respect. Indeed, they may instead lead one to conclude that it is best to privately and quietly order one's soul, mind ones' own business and gratefully live out one's life without tending to the political. That is, we are to **only** mind our own souls and turn away from the political. This is, however, very far from how we see Socrates living *his* life: he may not be at the assembly, busying himself with law-making. But he gives us an idea about the very real possibility of being political and "upsetting", as a private person, and an educator[66]. He makes us see that politics does not, and *should* not exist only in the public sphere: All of life is to varying extents political, including the life of the soul.

---

[65] Deneen, *Democratic Faith*, 2005 p197.
[66] On my reading Socrates is political: his discussion and inquiries, his "what is it" questions are controversial, and sometimes upsetting.

In my view therefore, the city in speech does not **only** fall apart to make us remember that the real topic of examination and concern is the soul. Instead, I agree with Allan Bloom, that the city in speech **also** falls apart to show us the dangers of social utopianism and radical idealism[67]. The city in speech is an example of **one** ideal, in this case justice, taken to its very extreme, without consideration for any other ideals or goods, in **both** city and soul. Instead of encouraging us to create little police-states and "police-souls", Plato is instead warning us as to what can happen if we take an ideal to its farthest limit, without appropriately balancing it with other ideals, or with the actual and practical.

The city in speech is thus an investigation into the nature and function of justice in both the city and the soul. Justice is one of the conventionally recognized virtues, and it needs to be investigated because even though many people *believe* to know what it is[68] , as we see in the *Republic,* this mostly turns out to be false. Justice is of utmost relevance and concern, however, it is not the only ideal or excellence, nor is it, as we shall see shortly, the "highest" ideal, and the person who takes it to be is mistaken. To take this road one either ends up believing that the only possible life for the philosopher is to turn away from the world, or that one could, driven by idealistic fervour, imitate the city in speech here on earth. Both are equally unproductive; and both roads make Plato an extremist or fanatic[69]. To have **only** perfect justice, in the city and the soul, is to sacrifice not only poetry, freedom, privacy, diversity, and novelty, but even love and philosophy.

Still, if Plato wanted to stress the dangers of utopias and one-sided idealism, is this a good way to go about it? In my view, it is: Plato **does** succeed in illustrating quite effectively the unattractive aspects and dangers with radical idealism. The angry accusations from freedom and democracy-minded readers attest to this. The just city is upsetting, and at first, we may feel insulted: believing that we are far more "progressive" and tolerant than to obediently swallow Plato's elitist dogma. This upsetting aspect is, I think, very deliberate: this is Plato's way of "stinging" his readers into doing philosophy

---

[67] The *Republic*, Allan Bloom Interpretative Essay, p256.
[68] For example, Cephalus, Thrasymachus, and Polemarchus.
[69] Randall, *Plato Dramatist*, 1965 p160.

in much the same way as Socrates goes about upsetting many of his fellow citizens in Athens. And even though the city in speech as a final image is too extreme, it is not without value. It helps to bring the idea of justice to life, and it draws out and illustrates the implications of uncompromising perfection. However, the *Republic* does not only teach us about the dangers of extreme idealism. We also learn about justice and philosophy in a more positive, practical way. For instance, we see that we cannot begin to understand what justice is unless we know what justice is *not*. Finding out what different people *think* justice is, is therefore highly valuable. It is the first step in any fruitful philosophic discussion, and it allows for the possibility of criticism and revision of beliefs and opinions. Secondly, we also see that there is no reason to give up or be let down if an ideal falls apart.

Yet perhaps Plato's critique is also more specific and direct? In other words, perhaps he is not only critiquing social idealism in general? John Herman Randall argues that in presenting the just city Plato is actually defending the Athenian ideal against Sparta. Plato recognized Sparta's superior efficiency and military organization, however, in Sparta "organization takes precedence even over the life of *theória*, of imaginative insight …there are much better philosophers in imperfect states… better art, better poetry, better life, better men – better everything but Justice or efficient organization"[70]. I am inclined to agree with Randall: to be *only* just, or *only* courageous, is too extreme. Sparta may be a more efficient society than Athens but it is not the optimum replacement for a corrupt democracy[71]. The efficiently organized life is **not** the best life, which leads me to the next key image relating to the ideal: the idea of the Good.

The Sun: child of the Good

Above justice, courage, self-control and the other excellences is the idea of the Good, discussed at length in Book 6 immediately preceding and introducing the image of the divided line. What sets the good apart from, for instance, the just or the beautiful? While the beautiful may be deemed satisfied with appearances or that which *seems* to be a certain way even if is not, the good is **not** like this: "when it comes to good things, noone

---

[70] Randall, *Plato Dramatist,* 1965 p171.
[71] Sparta had defeated Athens in the Peloponnesian War, it would make sense for Athens to turn to Sparta and see what the causes of their military success are, see Randall *Plato Dramatist*, p170.

is satisfied with what is opined to be so but each seeks the things that *are"*(505d). In other words, we may desire that which seems just and beautiful, but we do not desire that which is not, but only *seems* good[72]. The idea of the good is the **standard** against which we measure and carry out our actions. If I wish to *seem* just, I do not seek this reputation because I think it will be bad for me[73].

But, as Socrates remarks, the problem is that most of us are not able to define and gain any 'stable trust" (505e) into what the good really **is**. Justice, courage, beauty, friendship, self-control etc are only of importance if they are good, and with only very insecure or vague opinions of what the good consists of, "this drags down any knowledge we may have about the other excellences" (505d-e). Nonetheless, *even* if people often are either unable to define the notion of the good, or simply refer to it as that which produces pleasure, the good, in some shape or form, is of **supreme** importance to us. If we take away the good, all else loses meaning[74]. However, among all of Socrates' "what is it" - questions, the one concerning the good is perhaps the most difficult one to answer. How do we define the good? Yet one could argue that even if we are unable to completely define what the good is, intuitively it is possible to possess at least partial knowledge as to whether something is good or bad. In other words, it is possible to have an idea of the good *without* providing one all-encompassing definition.

As it turns out it is not possible for Socrates to tell Glaucon directly what the good is either: even though Glaucon is ever so persistent in pushing him to do so (506c-d). It is too difficult for Socrates to share his opinions on the nature of the good so he turns to an image: the sun, off-spring of the good (506e). However, Socrates cautions Glaucon that

---

[72] It is true that Glaucon wants justice to be good *without* regard to appearances. However, the point is that as Socrates says: "many men would choose to do, possess and enjoy the reputation for things that are opined to be just and fair, even if they aren't" (505d). This is **not** the case with the idea of the good.
[73] Roochnik, *Beautiful City*, 2003 p 67.
[74] Yet, it could be objected that Socrates is foolish since he does not take into account the fact that sometimes we are of weak will: we know that something is bad for us yet we do it anyway, addiction, for instance would be one of these examples. However, I do not think that the notion of the good is wholly absent even under these circumstances; the addict nevertheless is seeking some sort of good, albeit be it temporary or entirely physical. If there was no perceived goodness at all in any of our activities, would we do them?

this child of the good is only a *sliver* of the good itself: it is only the "interest" (507a), and Glaucon needs to keep this in mind, so as not to mistake the sun for the good (507a). The image of the sun portrays the good to have the same relationship to intelligence as the sun does to sight and that which is seen. The good is thus not intelligence: just like sight and light is not the sun (508b). Likewise, even though the good is related to knowledge and beauty it is not that which it **is** "just as in the other region it is right to hold light and sight sun-like, but to believe them to be sun is not right; so too, here, to hold these two to be like the good is right, but to believe either of them is the good is not right" (509a).

The image of the sun illustrates the *overarching* importance of the idea of the good. Without the sun there is no possibility of life. Likewise, absence of the good spells only death for the soul. Sight, growth, warmth etc are not possible without the sun, and similarly, none of the excellences, such as justice, friendship, moderation, courage etc have any meaning or real "life" without the idea of the good. The image of the sun *impresses* the extreme importance of the good on us in a more powerful fashion than if Socrates had simply described the good without this image. It makes us **see**, not only that the idea of the good is important, but just *how* important it is in relation to everything else. At the same time we are also reminded that all Socrates can give us is a sliver of the good, a rather poor or narrow image: so brilliant is the idea of the good. Again, it helps to picture the sun. Just as we are unable to stare directly at the sun without being blinded, we also have to make do with an *image* of the good. On my reading, the discussion of the good is therefore enriched by the parallel to the sun. The image leaves us with something concrete: we can remember that the good is *like* the sun, and that it brings light and life to the soul.

Furthermore, for my purposes it is essential that when Plato brings in his most important and complex idea, the idea of the good, images are not abandoned. Instead, in philosophic discussion images are an important way in which we can share complex opinions about essential, abstract, ethical ideas. To me, this destabilizes the supposition that as far as the "higher" philosophical issues are concerned, the true rational philosopher is completely freed from the imagination and images[75]. Indeed, **even** if this is the case when the philosopher thinks, which is almost impossible to know for a fact, it is not the case in discussion. The use of metaphors, elaborate images and myths at crucial points in the text, indicate a close relationship between ideas, images and philosophy. Images are important because rather than providing us with "set" or easy definitions, they inspire us to search for ourselves.

Weaving the Good Life

Socrates' image of the good does not provide a clear or straightforward idea of what the good is. But it inspires us to question and search for it ourselves. However, even if Plato does not come out and tell us exactly what the good is he *does* show us important aspects of the good **life**. The good life is not life in the city in speech, nor is it a life where one only buries one's head in the clouds in search for metaphysical definitions; the good life is not asceticism, it is not hedonism. Instead, the good life is the **harmony** of all the excellences and, however important justice is, it needs to be incorporated into this harmony[76].

On my reading, the good life, which in the *Philebus* is referred to as the "mixed" life (66a-c)[77], while not laid out as plainly in the *Republic* it is not only centered around the discussion of the idea of the good in Book 6; it is also hinted at by Socrates' recurring references to music and weaving[78]. Both arts, if performed in a *graceful* manner require balance, variation and harmony: high notes mixed with low ones, the weavers' mix of colours and materials blended in a beautiful garment. In life, this takes the expression of a constant blending or weaving of the high and low; the ideal and the actual, the earthy and the divine. The balancing of justice, courage, friendship, self-control, eros, speech and deed: **this** is the good life. There is no clear formula, or exact proportions for this life. As

---

[75] This is one possible interpretation of the image of the Divided Line in Book 6.
[76] Randall, *Plato Dramatist,* 1965 p163.
[77] It is referred to as mixed because it contains *both* thought and pleasure and the resulting harmony is the good. Plato, *Philebus* trans. and intro Dorothea Frede (Indianapolis: Hackett publishing Company) 1993, See 66a-c.
[78] In the *Republic*, Socrates connects graceful music to the virtues by likening it to moderation, see 402b-c. Further, Socrates also speaks of the need to harmonize and balance activities and education: the guardians are to **harmonize** music and gymnastics, see 410e.

the myth of the soul's journey in the *Phaedrus* reminds us, we only have partial sight as humans (248a); in this regard we are doomed to a life of imperfection. However, this does not mean that we should not strive and search for better and more stable knowledge about our souls and our world[79]. Music and weaving are thus metaphors for how we can harmonize and balance our souls.

To elaborate: Plato mixes the ideal with the earthy. For example, Socrates' speech in the *Symposium*, where he is praising an ideal and at times almost incomprehensible philosophic eros, is immediately followed by the entrance of Alcibiades who has a crush on Socrates. The abstract and remote ladder one has to climb to reach life with Supreme Beauty (215a) is framed by something very physical, tangible and comical: the roaring entrance of drunken, loud and excessive Alcibiades who demands to be led to Agathon (212d)[80]. Yet as Richard Hunter points out, the two speeches are not as different as one may first suppose[81]. The split between the earthy and the divine is not a clean split: they do not only illuminate one another, they exist within one another. Socrates and Alcibiades speeches both aim at telling the truth (198d; 215a), and even though Alcibiades' speech portrays a very physical love and longing, in his desire to make love to Socrates, it also contains references to the ideal. Alcibiades likens Socrates to an image of a Silenus[82] who when he is opened up reveals statues or images of gods (215b). However, this divinity is not easy to access, which harks back to the hint at impossibility of humans ever spending time with Supreme Beauty in Diotima's speech (212a). It also brings up the recurring theme of not mistaking seeming with being: Socrates is compared to an ugly Silenus or satyr, but *within* him resides brilliant beauty, in the shape of images of gods or virtues[83]. Thus, despite Socrates physical appearance, despite his fondness of

---

[79] For the importance of striving, see also Book 5 of the *Republic*, 490b.
[80] Richard Hunter points out that Alcibiades first sentence is a pun on Socrates speech because he demands to be led to Agathon, which immediately follows Diotima's prescription of how one will be led to the truly good (*agathon*) *Plato's Symposium* (New York: Oxford University Press) 2004, p98.
[81] Ibid., p99.
[82] Silenus is "the teacher and companion of the wine-god Dionysus. A notorious consumer of wine, he is usually totally drunk and is supported by satyrs or carried by a donkey…He has much wisdom and if captured by mortals he can reveal important secrets. Silenus is usually portrayed as a plump jovial old man with a long beard and stump nose, bald with a horse's tail" , "Silenus" Encyclopedia Mythica Online http://www.pantheon.org/articles/s/silenus.html.
[83] Hunter, *Plato's Symposium*, 2004 p100.

irony, there is great seriousness, divinity and beauty within him (216e). Alcibiades seems to know that it is good for him to be near Socrates, that he *should* be near him. However, he has not understood **how** he can learn from Socrates[84]. It is not simply a matter of getting close to Socrates, to become initiated and have him reveal *the* secret. His power does not "rub off" in this manner. The life of philosophy is to learn to think for oneself. Unlike the poets or the prophets, Socrates is not seeking to spellbind: his approach is self-conscious, it draws attention to what he is doing, what he assumes, and what he does not know. It invites others to join in, not as sheepish followers, but as critical participants.

To close the first part of this section: the ideal is important *even if* we can only partially access it, and the use of images is a central part of the ideal. The city in speech is an *imaginary vision* of justice: it is what can happen if the imagination is given free reign in speech[85]. Through images one can come to truly **see** the ideal and its wider implications. This seeing, this imaginary insight is what moulds the ideal in speech. There is also immense freedom in the imaginary activity of moulding an ideal in speech: it is to be permitted to engage in free association without boundaries and restrictions, which is one clear advantage speech has over deed. On the whole, the ideal is the continuous call urging us not to settle, but rather to keep striving and searching[86]. Yet the ideal is only **one** part of what it means to be human: to have an ideal in speech is **not** to be an ideal[87]. In other words, we have ideals; we strive, not to be released, but to lead a better life here and now. Ideals are useful, and a vital part of the search to better one's life.

Democracy: Collective Image-Making

It may seem an improbable and fantastical stretch to propose that there is a democratic connection to images and image-making in the *Republic*. After all, the setting of the drama consists of Socrates speaking to some privileged aristocratic Athenian youths, a very select crowd, to be sure. In fact, these aristocratic youths, along with some sophists

---

[84] Ibid., p101.
[85] Randall, *Plato Dramatist*, 1965 p163.
[86] On my reading, Socrates as an image of philosophy illustrates this type of striving, indicating that philosophy does not have an end, it never stops, see for example Book 5 490b.
[87] Randall, *Plato Dramatist*, 1965 p163.

rhapsodes, and foreigners appear to be for the most part the only people who have the time and interest to speak with and listen to Socrates. Other people are most likely too old (like Cephalus in Book 1) or too busy working and bringing up children. Philosophy from this view point appears to be an activity reserved for the wealthy few, with enough time to waste to dream up ideal cities in speech. What does this have to do with democracy?

I am not suggesting that philosophic discussion and image-making somehow are equivalent to the democratic notion of one-person one vote; and I am not suggesting that philosophy is democratic in the sense that it is for everybody all the time. If Socrates is the embodiment of the life of philosophy, it is an extreme life because we only ever see Socrates doing philosophy. We know from for instance, the *Symposium* that he went to war, that he exercises, that he has a family etc: yet we see him **only** engaged in philosophic discussion[88]. It is not a plausible life for most of us. It is too exhausting, upsetting and time-consuming to question, search, judge, critique, talk and think *all* of the time. But Plato is suggesting that if we never do it then we are making a big mistake, and it is in this dangerous complacency that we become either self-righteous or resign ourselves to the way things "are". Recall once again Socrates' words to Meno: "as long as we think we should search for what we don't know we'll be better people – less fainthearted and less lazy" (86b). Therefore, on my reading, it is not a waste of time to make images and dream up cities in speech. Still: how is this related to and helpful for democracy?

Firstly, I am suggesting that truthful discussion is democratic because each participant has a chance to both ask questions and to voice his or her opinions. In discussion we are allowed to clarify, restate, revise and continually modify our ideas. Further, we do not know exactly where a discussion will take us or where we will end up. These dynamic and open-ended aspects of discussion are dramatically illustrated in the *Republic*. The city in speech is the outcome of **collective** image-making; as such the ideal in the end reflects all of its participants, not only Socrates. It goes from the austere city of necessity (371e) to the feverish luxurious city (372e), to the purged city (399e), to the city in

---

[88] Peterman, *On Plato,* 2000 p48.

"heaven" (592b). Glaucon, Adeimantus, Polemarchus, and Thrasymachus **all** influence the direction, scope and outcome of the image. Thus I believe that philosophic discussion in general and collective-image making in particular can be said to be democratic, not in terms of whether the ideal image itself is democratic, the city in speech clearly is not, but by way of the **process** of making that image.

Secondly, democracy even if it is far from perfect, is the regime where fruitful and free philosophic discussion is more likely to exist. In Book 8 democracy is characterized by freedom, (557b); by diversity (557-c-d); and it is also regarded as "probably the fairest of the regimes" (557c). Furthermore, it is the place to be if one is looking for a specific regime because "it contains all species of regimes, and it is probably necessary for the man who wishes to organize a city, as we were just doing, to go to a city under a democracy"(557d). Adeimantus and Socrates also agree that democracy can be a sweet regime to live under because of its lack of compulsion (557e); and its compassion for those who have committed crimes (558a).Thus, despite being the second worst regime, superseded only by tyranny, on the scale of **justice**, it clearly also contains many other goods.

With regards to image-making, it is significant that Socrates says that it is in a democracy one should be if looking to found a city in speech. Democracy's corner-stones: diversity, tolerance and freedom open up the space for one to encounter, observe, compare and interact with all sorts of people and ideas. If one is searching for the ideal regime or soul it is the optimum place to be in. Yet democracy's diversity is not only good: its extreme negative outcome is that it will distract us too much and make us forget to question and distinguish, resulting in the free rein of relativity where anything goes, and any ranking or standards are abandoned (557c). In other words, if diversity becomes the *only* guiding principle, ideas and activities are deemed good solely based on being novel and people forget to judge and criticise. This life is the whimsical, non-serious life Socrates speaks of in Book 8: the democratic man looks to that which will divert and entertain him for the time being, doing a little bit of everything "and there is neither order nor necessity in his life" (561d). This is a careless life, and it illustrates how the "multicoloured cloak" of democracy can be distracting in its dazzling beauty, which is why I will now turn to the significance of **criticism** to philosophy and to democracy.

Criticism and Democracy

Peterman likens the central aspects of philosophy to the life, death and reincarnation of ideas[89]. The life of ideas requires democracy and the death of ideas requires criticism[90]. Death and dying in philosophy happens when we are courageous and willing enough to offer our ideas for criticism[91]. If we stubbornly cling to our ideas and beliefs we block the birth of new ones, and if we do not let ideas live in a democratic space we drastically narrow down the scope and birth of new ideas and the possibility of finding the best ones. Reincarnation or deathlessness in the realm of ideas happens when we realize that ideas need to be replaced with better ones, that they need to be revised, reviewed and remade[92].

To me, the journey in the *Republic* illustrates this birth, life and death of ideas. Socrates does not block criticism: he invites the others to join him in the search for justice. And he is not dismayed when the city in speech falls apart. As such the *Republic* is a magnificent image not only of justice, but of philosophy, dramatizing the search for knowledge and truth. But at the same time it is *only* an image, when we read the dialogue we can catch a glimpse of philosophy but it can never be a substitute for doing philosophy ourselves. The layers upon layers of possible meanings tied to the image of philosophy and justice in the *Republic*, the endless ways in which the text can be read, is Plato's call for us to begin to question, discuss, judge and criticise for ourselves

If criticism is the engine of philosophy it is also what links philosophy to democratic practices. Under many other regimes, especially the ones which are highly un-free, the spirit of criticism is stifled. For instance, the notion of what the good, and the good life consists of is not to be discussed because it has already been decided: in a tyranny, the good is the tyrant's desires, in an oligarchy, the good is the wealth of the few etc. In a

---

[89] Peterman, *On Plato*, 2000 p56.
[90] Ibid., p57.
[91] An example of this invitation to criticism is Socrates challenge to the poets in Book 10.
[92] Peterman, *On Plato*, 2000 p45.

democracy, however, the question of what is, and what is not ethically good is not off-limits for discussion[93]. There exists both a context and a space for philosophic discussion, and philosophy can, by continually criticising a democratic regime, help to keep a spirit of questioning and critical judgment alive.

I end this section now with a few words about images and image-making with regards to democracy. To summarize briefly: the many images in the *Republic* are not linked to democracy because they are all somehow democratic. Further, I am not suggesting that the imagination is democratic, or that a society will become democratic by solely focusing on the power of images and image-making. Instead I am proposing that images, and image-making, as a vital part of *philosophic discussion* are linked to democracy through philosophy's need for freedom of speech and pluralism in the world of ideas. Only those images in speech that are allowed to span across the whole spectrum of possibilities are **truly** useful to philosophy. Remove some of the freedom, or impose limits on collective image-making, and the image will be stifled and flat. The imagination is what allows us to think, see and express that which may at first seem utterly improbable or mad. Both philosophy and democracy need freedom of speech and pluralism to flourish and these activities in turn are sustained by the imagination, which helps us to negotiate, entertain, "see" and synthesize the plurality of viewpoints in discussion.

---

[93] Peterman, *On Plato*, 2000 p54.

V. Conclusion
Images and philosophy

In this paper I have argued that Plato reserves an important place and function for images in philosophic discussion. Image-making in the *Republic* is dynamic and social because it is collective. Socrates and his interlocutors found a city in speech **together,** in search for justice. This activity is both democratic and political because the image itself reflects the input of all the participants, and the act of pretending to be a founder of a city produces imaginative identification with the political, in this case the crafting of a city.

However, not **all** images are good. A key strength with Plato's treatment of images is that he also shows us how images can be bad. Images unaccompanied by rational argumentation, criticism, ranking and revision are not useful. To be useful to philosophy images belong firmly **in discussion**. As such they must also conform to a spirit of truthfulness. Images are not crafted and presented as an end in themselves where all that matters is that they dazzle and mesmerize their audience. An image such as Agathon's praise or Eros in the *Symposium*, is thus of no use unless it is "reined in" by critical questioning. It does not matter that Agathon's image **sounds** ever so beautiful. On the whole, bad images are thus those which are not *contained* within discussion, and those which help foster either complete relativity, false objectivity or an unnecessary wallowing in the tragic aspects of existence.

Good images in discussion are Plato's own fantastical images and myths. They engage and impress a point upon us, give us hope or help to awaken the passion for philosophy. They enrich, expand and balance rational argumentation and allow us to test, see and synthesize our ideas. They act as a medium for making abstract and ethical ideas more visible. A collective image in speech can be an important way in which we can learn about notions of the ideal. In the *Republic* we see not only justice come alive, but also its wider implications. In the end we see the dangers and sacrifices involved in taking an ideal to its extreme.

Democracy and Philosophy

But why does this really matter? How are images politically relevant and of use for us today? I have sought to illustrate that democracy **needs** images: to envision how things could be better, and to mediate between the ideal and the actual. Democracy thus needs images and image-making **in** philosophic discussion to keep striving for betterment, to not lapse into relativity or false objectivity. The essential link between images in discussion and more generally between democracy and philosophy, is criticism. A spirit of criticism is the engine of fruitful philosophic discussion, and this spirit is more likely to thrive and flourish in a democratic context and space marked by freedom of speech, diversity and tolerance. This democratic atmosphere is crucial for philosophy's search and constant striving for better ideas, better opinion and more stable knowledge. In the end images are thus relevant and political **because** of their important place in philosophic discussion.

Bibliography

"Ate" *Encyclopedia Mythica* from Encyclopedia Mythica Online
http://www.pantheon.org/articles/a/ate.html

Bundy, Murray Wright *The theory of Imagination in Classical and Mediaeval Thought* University of Illinois studies in language and literature. vol. 12, no. 2-3, 1927

Bernadete, Seth *On Plato's Symposium-Über Platons Symposion* (München: Carl Friedrich von Siemens Stiftung) 1994

Chambliss, J.J. *Imagination and reason in Plato, Aristotle, Vico, Rousseau, and Keats* (The Hague: Martinus Nijhoff), 1974

Corrigan, Kevin and Elena Glazov-Corrigan *Plato's Dialectic at Play: Argument Structure and Myth in the Symposium* (University Park, Pennsylvania: The Pennsylvania State University Press) 2004

Deneen, Patrick J. *Democratic Faith* (Princeton, New Jersey: Princeton University Press) 2005

Dodds, E.R *The Greeks and the Irrational* (Berkley: University of California Press) 1971

Elias, Julius A. *Plato's Defence of Poetry* (Albany: State University of New York Press) 1984

Halliwell, Stephen "Plato, Imagination and Romanticism" *The Passionate Intellect: Essays on the Transformation of the Classical Tradition,* ed. L. Ayres (New Brunswick, NJ: Transaction Publishers) 1995, pp23-37.

Halliwell, Stephen *The Aesthetics of Mimesis* (Princeton: Princeton University Press) 2002

Hart, Ray L. "Imagination in Plato" *International Philosophical Quarterly* Vol. V (1965) 436-461

Hunter, Richard *Plato's Symposium* (New York: Oxford University Press) 2004

Klein, Jacob *A Commentary on Plato's Meno* (North Carolina: The University of North Carolina Press) 1965

Kuhn Thomas, *The Essential Tension* (Chicago: Chicago University) 1977, p xii.

Monoson, Sara S. *Plato's Democratic Entanglements* (Princeton, New Jersey: Princeton University Press) 2000

Murdoch, Iris Existentialists and Mystics (New York: Allen Lane the Penguin Press) 1998

Nehamas, Alexander *Virtues of Authenticity: Essays on Plato and Socrates* (Princeton, New Jersey: Princeton University Press) 1999

Peterman, John E *On Plato* (Belmont, CA: Wadsworth), 2000.

Plato, *Euthyphro, Apology, Crito* trans. F.J. Church (New York: Macmillan Publishing Company) 1948

Plato, *Meno And Other Dialogues* trans. Robin Waterfield (New York: Oxford University Press) 2005

Plato, *Phaedo* trans. G.M.A. Grube (Indianapolis, Indiana: Hackett Publishing Company) 1977

Plato, *Phaedrus* trans and intro by James H. Nichols Jr. (Ithaca: Cornell University Press) 1998

Plato, *Phaedrus and Letters VII and VIII* trans. Walter Hamilton (London: Penguin Books) 1973

Plato, *Philebus* trans. and intro Dorothea Frede (Indianapolis: Hackett publishing Company) 1993

Plato, *The Republic* intro, trans., and notes by Allan Bloom (New York: Basic Books), 1968

Plato, *Sophist* trans. Nicholas P. White (Indianapolis; Hackett Publishing Company) 1993

Plato *The Symposium of Plato: The Shelley Translation* ed. and intro. by David O'Connor (South Bend, Indiana: St. Augustine's Press) 2002

Randall, John Herman Jr. *Plato Dramatist of the Life of Reason* (New York: Columbia University Press) 1970

Roochnik, David *The Tragedy of Reason* (New York: Routledge) 1990

Roochnik, David *Retrieving the Ancients* (Malden, MA: Blackwell Publishing) 2004

Roochnik, David *Beautiful City: The Dialectical Character of Plato's Republic* (Ithaca, New York: Cornell University Press) 2003

Shelley, Percy Bysshe "Defence of Poetry" in *The Four Ages of Poetry* ed. H.F.B Brett-Smith (Oxford: Basil Blackwell) 1953

"Silenus" Encyclopaedia Mythica at http://www.pantheon.org/articles/s/silenus.html

Strauss, Leo *On Plato's Symposium* ed. Seth Bernadete (Chicago: The University of Chicago Press) 2001

Taylor, C.C.W. *Socrates: A Very Short Introduction* (New York: Oxford University Press) 1998

Thayer, H.S. "Plato on the Morality of Imagination" *The Review of Metaphysics* Vol. 30 No. 4 Issue 120 (1977) 594-618

Watson, G "Discovering the Imagination: *Platonists and Stoics on* Phantasia" *The Question of "Eclecticism": Studies in Later Greek Philosophy* ed. John M. Dillon and A.A. Long (Berkley: University of California Press) 1988

Woodruff, Paul *First Democracy: The Challenge of an Ancient idea* (Oxford: Oxford University Press) 2005

www.ingramcontent.com/pod-product-compliance
Lightning Source LLC
Chambersburg PA
CBHW071415290426
44108CB00014B/1836